Sailors' Language

A Collection of Sea-terms and their Definitions

William Clark Russell

"In short, what with *dead-eyes* and *shrouds*, *cats* and *cat-blocks*, *dolphins* and *dolphin-strikers*, *whips* and *puddings*, I was so puzzled with what I heard that I was about to leave the deck in absolute despair. 'And, Mr. Chucks, recollect this afternoon that you *bleed* all the *buoys*.'"—*Peter Simple*.

Solis Press

PUBLISHER'S NOTE

The footnotes and appendix have been added by the publisher in this 2015 edition for clarification and information.

OF RELATED INTEREST FROM SOLIS PRESS

Also by William Clark Russell:
The Wreck of the "Grosvenor"
List, Ye Landsmen!
A Nightmare of the Doldrums

By Richard Henry Dana Jr.:
Two Years Before the Mast

By Gerard Wells:
Naval Customs and Traditions

Caution: this book was first published in 1883 and contains words and language that might offend

First published in 1883. This amended edition published by Solis Press, 2015

Typographical arrangement copyright © Solis Press 2015

Cover images:
Group portrait of the crew of the HMS *Cormorant* at Esquimalt, *c.*1888.
Anchor image designed by Freepik.com

All rights reserved. No part of this publication may be reproduced, stored in a retrieval system, or transmitted, in any form or by any means, electronic, mechanical, photocopying, recording or otherwise, except as permitted by the UK Copyright, Designs and Patents Act 1988, without the prior permission of the publisher.

This book is sold subject to the condition that it shall not, by way or trade or otherwise, be lent, resold, hired out or otherwise circulated without the publisher's prior consent in any form of binding or cover other than in which it is published and without a similar condition including this condition being imposed on the subsequent purchaser.

ISBN: 978-1-910146-13-2

Published by Solis Press, PO Box 482,
Tunbridge Wells TN2 9QT, Kent, England

Web: www.solispress.com | *Twitter*: @SolisPress

Contents

Publisher's note 2

Preface 4

A–Z listing 11–152

Appendix: A ship's sails *and* Four types of ship 153

Preface

This little volume is the fruits of an occasional spell of leisure. It is offered to the public because many might be glad to possess a cheap book of convenient size that would enable them to satisfy themselves without trouble about the meaning of nautical words often met with, but not always intelligible. I do not pretend that it is exhaustive—scores of words of which I may never have heard, are no doubt wanting; nor will I affirm that every term is accurately defined, though I have done my best to be exact. To make sure of this, however, and in order to enlarge the book beyond its present modest limits, I should be very thankful for suggestions and help in any shape. Sea-terms and definitions addressed to me, to the care of the publishers, will be gratefully received, and embodied in another edition, if called for. I am not acquainted with many nautical dictionaries. The marine glossaries are very meagre: even Dana's,[1] the best of them, belongs rather to the days when he was at sea—nearly half a century ago—than to this age of steamers and queer rigs. Admiral Smyth's[2] voluminous book is an immense collection of terms, but three-fourths of them have no more to do with sailor's language than have the words in Johnson's dictionary;[3] and the remainder is lacking in dozens of appellations now in vogue.

It was an article I contributed to a daily journal that put the idea of this volume into my head. That article will, I think, bear reprinting in this place, for I do not know that I could write anything better and more to the point as a Preface.

There is a well-known passage in *Peter Simple*,[4] in which Mr. Chucks, the boatswain, receives certain orders from the first lieutenant respecting mousings, turk's-heads, and goosenecks. "In short," says Peter, "what with dead-eyes and shrouds, cat and cat-blocks, dolphins and dolphin-strikers, whips and puddings, I was so puzzled with what I heard that I was about to leave the deck in absolute despair." He lingered long enough, however, to hear the lieutenant order Mr. Chucks to bleed all the buoys during the afternoon, a remark that drove the midshipman in terror into the cockpit. Others besides Peter Simple have been puzzled by sailors' language. Of all

---

1   Richard Henry Dana Jr. (1815–82), *The Seaman's Manual: containing a treatise on practical seamanship, a dictionary of sea terms, customs and usages of the merchant service, laws relating to the practical duties of master and mariners*, first published in 1841.
2   William Henry Smyth (1788–1865) *The Sailor's Word-Book: an alphabetical digest of nautical terms*, published in 1867.
3   Samuel Johnson (1709–84) *A Dictionary of the English Language*, published in 1755.
4   A novel written by Frederick Marryat (1792–1848) and published in 1834.

the various features of the procedure in marine courts of inquiry nothing is so curious as the bewilderment excited in the legal breast by the statements of the nautical witnesses. "We was going along all fluking when the wind drawed ahead. We trimmed sail, and in fore and mizzen-tor'garns'l, when a bit of a sea makin' her yaw, 'Mind yar luff, you soger,' sings out th' ole man, an' as he says this one of the jib-guys parted and sprung the boom, for ours wor spritsail gaffs, and the jib-guy and after-guy wor fitted in one, with a half-crown round the gaff end—are yar a followin' of me, sir?" If one could imagine a statement of this kind delivered to a lawyer, it might not be hard to figure the expression of face with which it would be received. What is a legal gentleman, whose knowledge of the sea is limited to a run from Dover to Calais when the Long Vacation gives him a spell of liberty, to make of such expressions as "boot-topping," "pazaree," "timenoguy," "Scotchman," "rombowline," "puddening," "leefange," and a hundred other words more bewildering still? And yet it is certain that if a sailor has to talk about his calling, he must use the language of the sea. There are no synonyms for "sister-blocks," "kevels," "sennit," "girt-line," "French-fake," and the rest of the vocabulary. If a lawyer cannot understand how the bight of a rope can be whipped into a snatch-block without passing the end through the sheave, there is nothing in language outside the terms of the marine statement of the process to enable him to master the sailor's meaning.

Indeed, sailors' talk is a dialect as distinct from ordinary English as Hindustanee[5] is, or Chinese. English words are used, but their signification is utterly remote from the meaning they have in shore parlance. A yard ashore means a bit of ground at the back of a house; at sea it is a spar. Every cabman knows what a whip is; but at sea it is a tackle formed by a single rope rove through a block. A traveller ashore is a well-known individual; but at sea he becomes an iron ring fitted so as to slip up and down a rope. A lizard is not a reptile, but a bit of rope with an iron thimble spliced into it, just as a bull is a small keg, and bees pieces of plank at the outer end of the bowsprit. Beating is not striking, but sailing by tacks; a bonnet is not for ladies' wear, but a piece of canvas laced to the foot of a jib; whilst a cat's-paw has as little to do with the feline animal as fiddles and harpings have with music.

Sailors' language, however, is by no means wholly compounded of the terms referring to the various parts of ships. Hardships and perils, cruel treatment, bad food, and the like, have imported a mass of rough sayings into the forecastle, many of which are sanctified by touches of rude poetry. Jack's ditties, too, are frequently vehicles of his emotions. When he does not

---

5   Called Hindi nowadays.

know how to "growl" fairly, he will put his feelings into a topsail-halliard song, and often has the anchor come up to a fierce chorus compounded of improvised abuse of the ship and the skipper, to which expression could not be given in a quieter method. A ship's carpenter once told me that he was clapped in irons and lay manacled for six weeks in a voyage to China for writing the words of a song which the sailors sang on every possible occasion when the captain was on deck. He gave me a copy of the words, which I found to be a rude enumeration of Jack's troubles, every stanza winding up with a shout of "Board of Trade,[6] ahoy!" Some of the verses are quite to the point. The first runs:—

> "I'm only a sailor man—tradesman would I were,
> For I've ever rued the day I became a tar;
> Rued the rambling notion, ever the decoy
> Unto such an awful life. Board of Trade, ahoy!"

One can imagine the skipper pricking up his ear at this shout, and looking very hard at the men who were chorusing it. The song goes on:—

> "I snubb'd skipper for bad grub, rotten flour to eat,
> Hard tack full of weevils; how demon chandlers cheat!
> Salt junk like mahogany, scurvying man and boy.
> Says he, 'Where's your remedy?' Board of Trade, ahoy!"

But worse follows:—

> "Can ye wonder mutiny, lubber-like, will work,
> In our mercantile marine, cramm'd with measly pork?
> Is it wonderful that men lose their native joy,
> With provisions maggoty? Board of Trade, ahoy!"

By this time, we may take it, the skipper was feeling about for a loose belaying-pin. But the exasperating touch was yet to come:—

> "Oh had we a crew to stand by when we're ashore,
> Show this horrid stuff that pigs even would abhor!
> Sue the swindling dealer who'd our health destroy.
> What say ye, oh sailor friends? Board of Trade, ahoy!
>
> "Dutchmen here before the mast, and behind it too!
> Dutchmen mate and carpenter, Dutchmen most the crew!
> Foreigners to man our ships, horrible employ!
> What's old England coming to? Board of Trade, ahoy!"

---

6   The part of the British government that regulated merchant ships at the time.

I quote these verses at length, as a fair sample of the sort of "growling" Jack puts into his songs. Unfortunately he is somewhat limited in melodies. Some of them are very plaintive, such as "The Plains of Mexico" and "Across the Western Ocean," and others have a merry, light-hearted go, such as "Run, let the bulljine run!" "Whisky, Johnny!" "Time for us to go," "I served my time in the Blackwall Line."

But the lack of variety is no obstruction to the sailor's poetical inspiration when he wants the "old man" to know his private opinions without expressing them to his face, and so the same "chantey," as the windlass or halliard chorus is called, furnishes the music to as many various indignant remonstrances as Jack can find injuries to sing about. The provisions have for years been a sore subject with the sailor. His beef and pork have earned more abuse from him than any other thing he goes to sea with. "What's for dinner to-day, Bill?" I remember hearing a sailor ask another. "Measles," was the answer, that being the man's name for the pork aboard his vessel. "Old horse," is the sailor's term for his salt beef; and some old rhymes perhaps explain the reason:—

> "Between the main-mast and the pumps
> There stands a cask of Irish junks;
> And if you won't believe it true,
> Look, and you'll see the hoof and shoe.
> Salt horse, salt horse, what brought you here,
> After carrying turf for so many a year,
> From Bantry Bay to Ballyack,
> Where you fell down and broke your back?
> With kicks, and thumps, and sore abuse,
> You're salted down for sailor's use.
> They eat your flesh and pick your bones,
> Then throw you over to Davy Jones."

Out of his sea fare, however, such as it is, Jack nevertheless manages to manufacture several dishes, of which the names are worthy of the contents and flavour. "Lobscouse," "dandy-funk," "dogsbody," "seapie," "choke-dog," "twice-laid," "hishee-hashee" are among some of the delectable entrées which the sailor contrives to get out of his kids. Whatever is at hand is popped into these messes; nothing comes amiss, "from a potato-paring to the heel of an old boot." Soup-and-bouilli is another standing sea-dish, and, taking it all round, is the most disgusting of the provisions served out to the merchant sailor. I have known many a strong stomach, made food-proof by years of pork eaten with molasses, and biscuit alive with worms, to be utterly capsized by the mere smell of soup-and-bouilli. Jack calls it "soap and bullion, one onion to a gallon of water," and this fairly expresses the character of the nauseous compound. Sea-puddings, as there is scarcely any variety that I know of among them, have not many names. "Duff" means a large lump of flour and grease boiled in a bag; "doughboys"—pronounced "doboys," the *o* broad—are the same flour and grease in small lumps. Dough jehovahs are a Yankee pudding, and worthy of the people who first taught the British sailor to eat pork with treacle. Bread in sailors' language means biscuits; the bread that landsmen eat is called by Jack "tommy" and "soft tack." Tea is "water bewitched," and no better title could be found for the pale yellow liquor thick with stalk-ends, which fills the sailor's hookpot when he goes to breakfast or supper.

It may be that the resentment kindled in the sailor's soul by the nature of the ship's stores induced him to extend his poetical imagination to all who had anything to do with the provisions, for assuredly the cook has not escaped. He is variously designated; sometimes he is "Drainings," sometimes "Slushy," and sometimes "Doctor," while the steward is called "Flunkey," and the steward's mate "Jack in the Dust." The carpenter is more politely termed "Chips," and "Sails" does duty for the sailmaker. Many an old prejudice survives in sea-language; as, for instance, the word "soger" (soldier), which is as strong a term of contempt as one sailor can fling at another, whilst "sogering" means to loaf, to skulk; as if in Jack's opinion loafing and skulking were characteristics of the soldier. "Lobster" is another of his terms for the military man, suggested, of course, by the red coat. The marine used to be Peter Pipeclay in the navy; I am ignorant whether the name is preserved; but another old term is to this day current among merchantmen, who will speak of a navy sailor as "Johnny Haultaut," in reference to the well-braced yards, the taut running rigging and the snug bunts of the man-of-war. The merchant seaman, however, has not escaped his own fertile invention, and does not apparently blush to figure as "Jack Muck" and "Shellback."

It is peculiar to the sailor to call all foreigners "Dutchmen." No matter whether a man be a Dane, a German, a Norwegian, a Swede, in Jack's estimation he is a "Dutchman." I once asked a sailor what he meant by a Dutchman. "Why," said he, "any man who says yaw for yes." This love of generic titles, no doubt, induces sailors to make the word "growl" stand for complaining, abusing, &c. If a man murmurs at the pea soup, he is "growling." If he mutters at being roused out in his watch below, he is "growling." Whether he grumbles under his breath or shouts at the skipper in a white fury, he is "growling." It is one of the most elastic words in the seaman's language. Many curious terms and expressions have found their way into the sea dialect. "Dowse the glim" is to put out the light; and "Dowse that, now," is a sailor's way of saying "Hold your tongue." To "tumble up" is to come out of the forecastle or any other part of the ship, and "lay down" is to descend from aloft. "All hands, tumble up! men, tumble up!" bawls the boatswain, thumping on the scuttle; and "Fore-topsail yard, there! lay down, d'ye hear?" are orders which do not seem to correspond with a landsman's notions of the things required to be done. Seamen are fond also of odd ejaculations, such as "Bully for you!" and "There she goes, boys! put another bit of beef in soak!" when the wind freshens up and the ship swings through it with a sharper plunge.

Another ejaculation on a like occasion is, "There she blows! whilst she creaks she holds!" "More beef!" is a cry often raised when men hauling on a rope find they want help. It means, "Tail on here more hands." Equally suggestive is the expression "A hurrah's nest, everything at top and nothing at bottom, like a midshipman's chest," intended to express the utmost state of disorder, when nothing wanted can be found. "Working Tom Cox's traverse—three times round the long boat and a pull at the scuttlebutt," signifies the behaviour of a man who is as slow in his work as he can be, out of spite for having been ill-treated, or from any other motive of resentment. Unpopular captains have suffered much from "Tom Cox's traverse;" when men sent aloft are always dropping their jobs, and coming down on pretence of having forgotten something; when the anchor is sluggishly raised and without a chorus; and when nothing is done with a will.

Other favourite expressions are "Handsomely over the bricks," that is, walk carefully, mind where you are going; "There are no half-laughs or purser's grins about me, mate—I'm right up and down like a yard of pump-water," used when a man wants to let the others know he is in downright earnest; "I'd weather him out, if he was the Devil himself," one meaning of which is, "I'll stick to the ship, let the skipper do his worst;" "It's a good dog nowadays that'll come when he's called, let alone coming before it," a sailor's excuse for not showing himself forward in stopping a mischief, for not choosing to act until he was ordered; "I didn't come through the cabin windows," that is, "I'm a sailor: I worked my way aft from forwards; I know my duty and am not going to be taught it;" "The girls have hold of the tow rope, and can't haul the slack in fast enough," when the ship is homeward-bound and sailing fast—an image full of rude poetry it always seemed to me; "He hasn't got the hayseed out of his hair," applied to a greenhorn from the country; though such is Jack's love of the country that "to sell a farm and go to sea" is a favourite expression of his to denote the very height of imbecility. "As independent as a wood sawyer's clerk" is a phrase, apparently of American origin; one may often hear it used among sailors. "I've been through the mill, ground, and bolted," is to assert immense experience, and the uselessness of anybody attempting to "try it on." To "know the ropes" is the same assertion qualified. "Every hair like a rope yarn," "Every finger a fishhook," "He hasn't a lazy bone in him," are all high compliments. Then there are scores of such phrases as "working their old iron up," "long togs," for shore-going clothes; "ride a man down like the maintack," to go on punishing him with plenty of hard work; "up keeleg," "paying a debt with the fore-top nil," namely, sailing away without paying; "cracking on," piling on canvas or keeping a ship under a heavy press in a strong wind; "an Irishman's hurricane—right up and down," a calm; "Davy putting on the coppers for the parson," the noise a tempest makes in approaching; "keep your weather-eye lifting," &c.

Of many sea-phrases the meaning is really so subtle as utterly to defy translation, whilst many fit the vocational conditions so accurately that any divergence from the exact expression will puzzle a seaman as much as if he was being ordered about in French. There are shades of signification in the terms which a man must go to sea as a sailor to understand. No books will give them. They are not to be mastered by listening to seamen talking. There would seem to a landsman no particular appropriateness in such a phrase for instance as "sleep in," though it somehow happens that at sea no other term would do. And the same thing may be said of such expressions as "to turn in all standing," meaning without removing your clothes. Any way, it is quite certain that to stop a sailor from telling his story in his own fashion is, to use his phrase, "to bring him up with a round turn;" and to expect him to find other words than those which occur naturally to him in relating incidents of a profession crowded with expressions to be heard nowhere except on board ship, is to put him upon a labour of definitions which even a Samuel Johnson would, I suspect, very promptly decline.

A

A. B.—The letters signifying able-bodied seaman or able seaman.

Aback.—A ship is said to be *aback* when the wind presses her sails backwards against the masts, so as to force her sternways or drive her bodily to leeward.

Abaft.—Anything behind another thing is called *abaft* it; as the wind is *abaft* the beam, the *galley* is abaft the foremast.

Able-bodied.—Healthy, strong, fit for duty.

Able seaman.—The rating of the best or head sailors of a crew, to distinguish them from ordinary seamen and boys.

Able-whackets.—A game of cards that used to be popular in the forecastle: when a man lost he was beaten over the hands.

Aboard.—On a ship. On board. It is the sailor's word for on board. Keep the land *aboard* is to keep it close.

About.—Newly tacked. "She has gone *about*" means that a vessel has gone round, head to wind, so as to bring the wind on the other bow.

Above-board.—Honest, fair, honourable in speaking or dealing. "I'll be above-board with you" means I'll be frank and tell you the truth.

Abox.—To brace the yards abox is to lay the fore-yards aback, or so brace them that they shall be against the wind.

Abrase.—To smooth down a plank.

Abreast.—Opposite to. Alongside of. "We brought up abreast of the lightship," that is, We dropped anchor so as to bring the lightship on a line with our beam.

Abrid.—A pintle-plate.

Abroach.—A barrel is abroach after it has been tapped for use.

Abstract log.—A copy of all the more important entries in the log-book.

Aburton.—The position of casks stowed athwartships; that is, from side to side across the hold.

Acast.—An old term for being cast away or shipwrecked on an island or a desolate shore. Yards are braced *acast* in weighing anchor, so as to cause the vessel to cant in a given direction.

Acater.—An old term for a ship-chandler, or rather one who furnished a ship with provisions.

Accommodation-ladder.—Steps at the gangway, over the side, to enable people to enter or leave a vessel. The ordinary name is gangway ladder. There are no stairs at sea; everything is steps or a ladder.

Ackman.—A person who commits piracies on fresh water.

A-cockbill.—When the yards are topped up at an angle with the deck. The anchor is said to be *cock-billed* when it hangs at the cat-head.

Acon.—A flat-bottomed boat used in the Mediterranean.

Acting commission.—A commission for filling the vacancy caused by the death of a naval officer on a station.

Acting order.—An order for filling up the vacancy caused by the invaliding of a naval officer.

Active service.—Serving against an enemy, whether in his presence or in his neighbourhood; serving on full pay.

Act of God.—A term indicating perils of the deep beyond human power to control or oppose, as when a ship is struck by lightning or founders in a storm, being tight and sea-worthy at the time and ably commanded.

Adjustment is the term for the settlement by an average-adjuster of the indemnity to be paid by the person who takes the risk to the person insured after the loss of the vessel

Adjustment of the compass.—The term for noting the errors of a ship's compass by swinging a ship so as to test the compass by various bearings.

Admiral.—The chief commander of a fleet.

Admiral of the Fleet is an honorary distinction, but it nevertheless renders the bearer of it the highest officer in the Royal Navy.

Adrift.—Broken loose. "She went adrift from her moorings" means the ropes or chains that held her parted and let her go loose.

Advance-note.—A note formerly given to merchant seamen in part payment of their wages. It differed from the Allotment-note (which see) in that it was made payable to the holder unless the seaman failed to proceed in his ship.

Advance-squadron.—Ships of war on the look-out.

Advice-boat.—A vessel employed in war-time for the transmission of intelligence.

Adze.—A kind of axe, having an arching blade set at right angle to the handle, and used by carpenters, coopers, &c.

Affair.—A word indicating an engagement, a fight at sea without decisive results.

Affreightment.—A contract of affreightment is the letting of the whole or part of a ship for cargo.

Afore.—The forward part of a ship. Sometimes used for *before*, as *afore* the mast.

Aft.—The hinder part of a ship; as, "The captain was aft," meaning he was on the quarter-deck or poop at the hinder end.

Aft-castle.—In olden times this was a kind of small round house or wooden structure on the hinder part of a fighting-ship.

After-body.—The name given to the form or shape of a ship from the middle or amidship part of her to the stern.

After-cloths.—The hindmost portions of fore and aft sails in which they are furled and which bring the seams up and down.

After-guard.—The hands stationed aft to work the sails there.

Afternoon watch.—The watch from noon until four p.m.

After-peak.—A portion of the hold in the after-part of a ship, corresponding with the fore-peak.

After-sails.—All the canvas on the main and mizzen-masts of a full-rigged ship and barque, and on the main-mast of a brig.

After-timbers.—All the timbers abaft the midship part of a ship.

After-yards.—The main and mizzen-yards of a full-rigged ship. The main-yards of a barque or brig.

Aground.—A vessel is said to be aground when she is ashore or held fast upon a shoal.

Ahead.—The forward part of a ship. Also in advance of a ship. The opposite of abaft.

Ahold.—An old word, signifying lying close to the wind, as we now say close-hauled.

Ahoy.—A call for attention from a person at a distance. As "Brig ahoy! where are you coming to?" "Ship ahoy!" "Hallo." "What ship is that?" &c.

A 1.—A character used in the classification of ships, and denoting vessels which have been built in accordance with certain rules. There are several of these characters, such as 100 A 1 90 A 1, 80 A 1, A 1 in red, Æ, Å, L 1, &c.

Air-cone.—A place in the marine engine for the reception of the gases from the hot well.

Air-ports.—Holes in a ship's bow for ventilating her.

Air-pump.—A part of a marine engine to take away the air and gases which come from the water in the boiler and which cannot be condensed.

Air-pump bucket valves.—Valves in the air-pump bucket opening upwards on the descent of the piston, and closing on the upward stroke, lifting water, &c., into the hot well.

A-lee.—Said of the helm when it is put down. "Helm's a-lee!" the warning in tacking a ship that the rudder is turned so as to bring the ship's head into the wind. "Hard a-lee!" means hard over, put the rudder as far as it will go to windward.

Alert.—Smartly alive and on the look-out. Alertness is a sure sign of a good seaman.

All aback!—A cry to denote that the wind is pressing the sails against the mast and stopping the progress of the vessel.

All ataunto!—Said of a ship when all her masts are aloft.

Allege.—A boat used in some French rivers and harbours for ballasting vessels.

All fluking.—Said of a ship that goes along sailing with the wind well abaft the beam, and the weather clew of the main-sail hauled up.

All gone!—A seaman's answer to the order "Let go!" when the order is obeyed.

All hands.—The whole of the crew of a vessel. When the watch below are summoned to help the watch on deck, the cry is always "All hands reef top-sails," "All hands shorten sail," or whatever may be the reason for which they are required.

All-hands work.—Work that requires the whole ship's company to perform it. Tacking, reefing top-sails, shortening sail in a sudden heavy squall, bringing up, getting under weigh, would be called all-hands work.

All in the wind.—Said when the sails are shaking through bad steering, or by a sudden swing and come-to of the ship that brings her head into the wind.

Allotment-note.—A note given to a merchant seaman in part payment of his wages, and made payable only to one of certain relations or a savings'-bank.

Allowance.—The quantity of provisions, water, rum, &c., served out to each man at sea.

All-standing.—Fully dressed. To turn in *all-standing*, is to go to bed with one's clothes on. Brought up all-standing, means to be taken unawares, to be brought to a stand suddenly.

Aloft.—On high. Any part of the masts is called aloft. To go aloft is to climb the rigging. It is also the sailor's word for heaven, as "His soul is gone aloft."

Alow.—A term sometimes, but very rarely used for *below*, and then perhaps only for the sake of alliteration, as "She had studding-sails aloft and alow."

Altitude.—An arch of a vertical circle intercepted between the centre of the object and the horizon.

Amain.—An old word signifying smartly, bear a hand.

Amidships.—The middle part of a vessel. Also a sea term for the middle part of anything.

Amplitude.—An arch of the horizon contained between the centre of the object when rising or setting, and the east or west points of the horizon.

Anchor.—The well-known iron implement which when dropped overboard with a chain or rope attached to it holds a ship. It consists of several parts, i.e. the ring, the beam or shank, the arms and flukes, and the stock.

Anchorage-dues.—A charge upon vessels entering or using a river, dock, creek, basin, &c.

Anchor-ball.—An explosive that was formerly attached to a grapnel, and exploded when the grapnel was thrown on to the enemy's side.

Anchor-buoy.—See *Buoys*.

Anchor-chocks are pieces of wood in which an anchor rests when stowed on deck.

Anchor-hoops.—Circular irons for connecting the stock to the end of the shank of an anchor.

Anchor-light.—A single bright light shown by a ship when at anchor.

Anchor-lining.—A protection on the side of a ship to prevent it from being injured by the bill of the anchor when hove up.

Anchor-stocking.—A term in ship-building expressive of a mode of working in planks with tapered ends.

Anchor-watch.—The name given to the look-out that is kept aboard a ship when she is anchored.

Ancient.—The old name for an ensign.

Anemometer.—An instrument for registering the pressure of wind.

Aneroid.—A metallic barometer that indicates by a hand the height at which mercury will stand in the barometer.

Angel's footstool.—An imaginary sail jokingly assumed to be carried by Yankee vessels. It is pretended to be a square sail and to top the sky-sails, moon-sails, cloud-cleaners, &c.

Angle-irons.—Bars of iron whose sections form two sides of a triangle, used for the ribs or frames of an iron ship.

Annular-piston.—A piston made in the form of a ring that encircles an inner cylinder enclosed by another. By this means the connecting-rod is lengthened.

Answer.—A ship *answers* her helm when she obeys the movement of her rudder.

Answering pennant.—A flag that is hoisted when it is necessary to show that a signal is understood.

Apeak.—The term to indicate when a ship's cable is nearly up and down with her bows and the anchor on the ground.

Apron.—A timber within the stem of a wooden ship for the reception of the plank of the bottom and the heels of the foremost timbers.

Arched squalls.—Bursts of wind so called because they rise with a black cloudy arch. They are encountered in the eastern seas.

Arm-chest.—A movable case or chest for holding a ship's small arms.

Arming.—The name given to tallow or soap that is placed in the hollow of a deep-sea lead so that the nature of the ground may be shown by the particles which adhere.

Armour-bolts.—Nut and screw bolts used in securing the armour-plates on ironclads.

Armour-clad.—The designation of a man-of-war that is rendered shot-proof by immensely thick steel or iron plates.

Armourer.—One whose duty it was to look after and keep in repair the ironwork about a ship.

Arm-rack.—A frame for receiving fire-arms.

Arms.—A term for any kind of weapon. Also, the projections at the bottom of the shank of an anchor.

Articles.—A ship's articles are the document in which are recorded the names and signatures of the crew, their wages, the food to be given, &c.

Artificial or spindle eye.—An eye in the end of a rope formed by hitching the yarns of the rope round a piece of wood and then scraping, marling, parcelling, and serving them.

Ascensional difference.—An arch of the equinoctial intercepted between the sun or a star's meridian and the point of the equinoctial that rises with the object.

Ashore.—A ship is said to be ashore when she takes the ground and sticks fast. To go ashore is to quit a ship or boat for the shore.

Ash-pit.—A portion of the furnace of a steamer below the fire-grate surface to allow air to get to the fire through the spaces between the iron bars, and also for receiving the ashes.

Asleep.—This word is applied to sails when sufficiently steadied by the wind to be prevented from flapping.

Aspic.—A twelve-pound gun used in olden times.

Astern.—Behind. Over a ship's stern and at a distance, as "The vessel was a league astern." Also in the direction of the stern. "Go astern," an order to the engine-room to reverse the engines.

Athwart.—Across. "Athwart our hawse" said of a ship crossing another's bows.

Athwart hawse.—Across a vessel's head.

Athwartships.—Across the ship. Also across anything.

Athwart the forefoot.—A cannon-ball fired athwart or across a vessel's forefoot was a peremptory signal for her to bring to.

Atrip.—An anchor is said to be *atrip* when, after heaving at the windlass, the crew have raised the anchor off the ground, and it hangs by the cable up and down.

Avast.—An order to stop hauling or heaving; pronounced 'vast. A word going out of fashion as used among seamen, who would formerly say "'Vast there!" meaning, Stop that talking. It is now confined to ship's work.

Average.—A term to express all losses and accidents to ships and cargoes which arise from perils of the sea, and for which underwriters have to pay.

Average-bond.—An agreement among consignees or owners of a cargo to pay any proportion of average.

Away aloft!—An order in the navy to the men to mount the rigging. In the merchant service it is customary to say "Jump aloft."

Away with it!—An order to lay hold of a tackle fall or any rope, and instead of hauling, walk away with it.

Awash.—Anything level with the water so that it is sometimes covered and sometimes left exposed is said to be awash.

Aweather.—The situation of the helm when put in the direction whence the wind blows, supposing that you are steering with a tiller.

Aweigh.—The anchor is said to be *aweigh* or *away* when it is lifted off the ground.

Awning.—A canvas shelter stretched over a deck or a boat.

Awning-decked.—This expression is not of old standing. It is meant to signify an iron vessel, the upper portion of whose sheer-strake plate is in line with the main deck beams, and that has a deck above the main deck.

Auxiliary screw.—The name given to a vessel fitted with a propeller that can be raised for sailing when not required; or lowered and connected for steaming.

Axial oscillation.—A term to indicate a pendulum-like movement of the central part of a storm.

Ay, ay, sir.—The orthodox reply to any order signifying that it will be obeyed.

Azimuth.—An arch of a vertical circle intercepted between the meridian of the place and the azimuth or vertical circles passing through the centre of any object.

Azimuth circles.—Great circles passing through the zenith and nadir.

Azimuth compass.—An instrument for finding the magnetic azimuth or amplitude of a heavenly object.

B

Babbing.—A name given to a method of luring crabs by bait, and then netting them.

Bac.—The name of a French ferry-boat.

Back.—This term is applied to the shifting of the wind when it changes by a movement against the sun, i.e. from left to right.

Back.—To back a sail is to brace a yard against the wind so as to press the canvas against the mast.

Back and fill is to alternately brace the yards against the wind and then forward to fill the sails. This is done in manoeuvring to get out of a narrow passage, &c.

Back-balance of eccentric is placed at the back of the eccentric pulley of a marine engine to balance it on the shaft.

Back-balance of slide-valves.—A weight at the end of the valve lever of a marine engine for balancing the slides.

Back-board.—A board in the stern sheets of a boat to support the back.

Back her!—An order to the engineer to drive a steamer backwards by reversing the action of the propeller or paddle-wheels.

Backing.—The woodwork behind armour-plates.

Back-lash.—The term applied to the shock or jar caused by two pieces of machinery, one of which gives motion to the other, coming together with a sudden blow.

Back-ropes.—Small leading-lines, grafted or hitched to the back of the cat and fish-hooks and long enough to reach from the rail to the water.

Back-staff.—A sea quadrant invented by Davis, the navigator, in the sixteenth century. It is usually called the cross-staff.

Backstay.—A rope to support a mast and leading down abaft it to the side of the vessel.

Back-sweep.—The hollow of the top timber of a frame.

Back water!—An order to drive a boat stem ways by the oars.

Baffling.—The wind is said to be baffling when it keeps constantly shifting from one adverse quarter to another.

Balanced-rudder.—A rudder pivoted on an extension of the keel instead of hanging to the stern-post.

Balance-reef.—A reef in a fore-and-aft sail. When the points of this reef are tied it makes the sail's shape nearly triangular.

Bale.—To throw out water from a boat. Also to wind up, as to bale up yarns. Also a large bundle of wool or cotton.

Bale-goods.—Bundles, such as wool, Manchester bales, &c., in contradistinction to cased goods.

Bale-slings.—Slings formed of a circle of rope passed round the object to be slung, one end of the bight of the circle being passed through the other.

Balk.—Straight young trees when cut down and squared.

Ballahoo.—A name for a West Indian clipper schooner. Apparently she may also be a brig, to judge from *The Cruise of the 'Midge'*.

Ballastage is the levying of a charge for supplying ships with ballast.

Ballast-tank.—A tank or compartment in the bottom of iron steamships, or sometimes in the fore and after parts of the vessel, for the storage of water to serve as ballast.

Ballast-irons are fitted to the bottom and sides of a ship when required, to reeve the ballast-boards through to prevent shifting.

Balloon jib.—A large jib made of light canvas and used by yachts in gentle winds.

Baltimore clippers.—Vessels built at Baltimore, famous for their speed. They were the first to set the example of increasing the length of a vessel to about six times her beam.

Bangles.—The hoops round a spar.

Banking.—Banking up fires is raking the coals to the back of the furnace to impede combustion, whilst at the same time it enables the engineer to be in readiness to get up steam.

Banyan day.—A term meaning a bad day, a disagreeable day. Derived from a custom of withholding meat from crews on certain days.

Barbette.—A ship that mounts guns which fire clear over the side, instead of through embrasures.

Barca-longa.—A Spanish lug-rigged vessel. Also a Spanish gunboat.

Barge.—A vessel rigged with or without a mast and a sprit-sail. Also a boat used by admirals and naval captains.

Bargee.—One of the crew of a barge or canal-boat.

Barge-mate.—The coxswain of a navy barge when the boat is occupied by a person of distinction.

Barge-men.—The crew of a navy barge.

Barget.—A small barge.

Bark.—A poetical term signifying any kind of vessel. So Byron: "My bark is on the sea." It is never used by sailors.

Bar keel.—An iron keel, made of massive bars united by scarphs.

Barkey.—A sailor's endearing term for the vessel he likes.

Barometer.—An instrument for showing the weight or pressure of the air.

Barometer chart.—A chart on which the indications of the barometer are shown every day for a month in lines.

Barque.—A three-masted vessel. The two forward masts are ship-rigged. The after or mizzen-mast is rigged with a spanker and gaff top-sail.

Barquentine.—A three-masted vessel rigged like a brig on the fore-mast, and like a schooner on the main and mizzen-mast.

Barratry.—A legal term to express any fraudulent act committed by a seaman to the prejudice of the owners of the vessel.

Barrel-bulk.—The space occupied by casks in a ship's hold.

Bar-shot.—Two half-shot united by a bar of iron and formerly used for dismantling a ship.

Base-board.—The name of a board having the numeral feet marked upon it, and used in taking the form of a ship when built.

Bateau.—A Canadian boat. Also a name for a pontoon.

Bathing-machine.—A name given to the old 10-gun brigs.

Batten down.—The hatches are said to be *battened down* when they are covered up with gratings or hatches, and tarpaulins which are secured by battens to prevent them from being washed away.

Battens.—Pieces of wood or iron placed round a hatchway to keep a tarpaulin over it in bad weather. Also pieces of wood fastened to the rigging to prevent it from being chafed.

Battering-ram.—A large piece of timber, armed at each end with iron caps and fitted with ropes. It is used for removing the angular blocks when a docked ship is sitting on them.

Battery.—A man-of-war's broadside armament.

Battledore.—The name of a movable iron arm in the cable-bitts.

Battle-lanterns.—Lanterns which formerly lighted the decks of a ship at night when in action, to enable the men to see what they were about.

Bawley.—A Thames shrimping vessel.

Beach-comber.—One who hangs about the shore on the look-out for jobs. It was chiefly applied to runaway seamen, deserters from whalers, who lived along the beach in South America, the South Sea Islands, &c. It is a term of contempt.

Beam.—That point of the sea or horizon which bears directly abreast of the midship section of a ship.

Beam-arms.—Curved ends of iron beams for joining them with the ship's side.

Beam-ends.—A ship is said to be on her beam-ends when she is so prostrated on her side by a hurricane or outfly of wind, or by shifting her cargo, as to submerge her lee rail.

Beam-engine.—A marine engine in which the reciprocating motion of the piston-rod is transferred through side rods and side levers to the connecting-rod, which by means of the crank continuously revolves the shaft.

Beams.—Those timbers in a ship which are placed across her to receive the decks.

Bear.—The situation of an object with reference to a ship, as, "How does the land bear?" in what direction is it by compass?

Bear.—An instrument for punching holes with the hand.

Bear a bob!—An expression signifying "look sharp."

Bear a hand!—An injunction to be quick, to look alive.

Bear away.—To alter the course so as to bring the wind more aft.

Bearding.—The part of the rudder that lies close to the stern post.

Bear down.—To approach an object from the weather side of it.

Bearers.—Cross bars in marine furnaces for supporting the ends of the fire-bars.

Bearing.—The bearing of anything is its situation with regard to the compass. As in speaking of a wreck, "Its bearings were E. half N."

Bearing-binnacle.—A small compass stand used in men-of-war.

Beating is sailing as nearly as the sails will allow in the direction whence the wind is blowing.

Beating the booby.—Said of a man when he is warming his hands by striking his breast.

Beat to quarters.—A roll on the drum as a signal for the crew to go to stations before an engagement.

Becalm.—To becalm a sail is to intercept the wind from it, as the fore-topsail is becalmed, when the wind is aft, by the main-topsail.

Becalmed.—A sailing-vessel is becalmed when the wind fails and leaves her motionless upon the sea.

Becket.—A handle made of rope.

Bed-bolt.—An iron bar on which the foremost end of the stool-bed of a gun-carriage rests.

Bedding.—The seating on which a boiler rests.

Bee.—A hook.

Beef.—"More beef!" an exclamation signifying that more help is wanted in pulling upon a rope, &c.

Beef-kid.—A tub into which the cook puts the men's meat when cooked, and which is carried into the forecastle.

Bees.—Wooden chocks on the bowsprit to reeve the fore-topmast stays through.

Beetle.—A hammer or mallet used in caulking.

Before the mast.—Living in the forecastle, serving as a "common sailor."

Behaviour.—A ship's behaviour is the quality she exhibits under various conditions of weather.

Belay.—To make a rope fast by taking a turn with it over a belaying-pin.

Belaying-pins.—Iron, brass, or wooden bars tapered, placed in holes in rails, hoops, &c., to make the running gear fast to.

Belfrey.—A frame from which a ship's bell hangs.

Bell-buoy.—A buoy with a bell inside or outside it, that rings as the buoy sways on the water. It is a fog or night signal.

Bell-rope.—A short rope spliced to a bell for striking the hours.

Bells.—The denoting of time on board ship. Eight bells signify noon or midnight, eight or four o'clock; half-past twelve, one bell; one o'clock, two bells; half-past one, three bells, and so on to eight bells. See Dog-watch.

Belly.—The full or round part of a sail when distended by the wind. Also the central cloths of a sail.

Belly-bands.—Bands of canvas across a sail to strengthen it for the reef-points.

Belly-guy.—A rope used in supporting the middle part of shears.

Belly-stay.—An extra support for a mast, secured half-way up it.

Bend.—To bend a sail is to attach it to the yard. Also a bend is a knot: to bend the end of a rope to another is to tie it to the other.

Bending-cradles.—Iron vertical frames fitted with transverse beams, and used for bending armour-plates for men-of-war to the required shape.

Benjie.—The name of a straw hat worn by sailors.

Bentinck.—A triangular-shaped lower sail.

Bentinck-boom.—A spar for stretching the foot of a square fore-sail.

Bentinck shrouds.—Ropes formerly used and extending from the futtock staves to the channels.

Berth.—A vessel's berth is the place where she lies alongside a wharf, quay, or pier, or at anchor; also, a berth is a sleeping-place on board a ship.

Berth decks.—The 'tween decks.

Berthing-rail.—A rail that formerly went round the head of a ship for the safety of the men when they were out on the head.

Best bower.—The larger of the anchors called the bowers.

Bethel.—A sailor's meeting-house.

Between decks.—Usually pronounced 'tween decks. The space between the main or upper, and the second lower decks.

Bezant.—A small Dutch yacht.

Bibbs.—The name given to timbers which are bolted to the hounds of a mast.

Bibles.—Small holy stones, no doubt originally so called because they oblige those who use them to kneel. They are also termed prayer-books for the same reason.

Bid-hook.—An old name for a small boat-hook.

Bight.—A bend or curve in a rope. Bring the two parts of a rope together, and you make a bight. Also a curve in a hawser or any other rope, though the parts be not together, is called a bight.

Bilboes.—Irons for securing a man's legs. This is an old term.

Bilge.—The largest circumference of a cask. Also the round of a vessel's bottom near the keel.

Bilged.—A vessel is said to be *bilged* when her bottom side is broken in by stranding.

Bilge-keels.—Projections on the edge of a keel and on the bilges.

Bilge-pumps.—Pumps for bringing the injection water from the ship's bilge instead of from the sea, in case of a leak.

Bilge-shores.—Timbers for supporting the bilge of a ship in a repairing dock.

Bilge-tank.—A tank with one of its lower edges cut off so that it may fit the ship's side.

Bilge-water.—The water that has collected, from one cause or another, in the bilge. Its unpleasant smell has made its name well known.

Bill.—The point at the extremity of the flukes of an anchor. It was formerly called the pea.

Bill-board.—A ledge of wood over the side to support the fluke of an anchor.

Bill of health.—A document certifying to the healthy condition of the ship and place when she left her last port.

Bill of lading.—An acknowledgment in writing by the master of a ship of the receipt of cargo and freight.

Bill tricing line.—A line secured to the bill of the hook of the block of a yard-tackle for tricing it up to the lower rigging.

Billy boy.—A vessel like a galliot, with two masts, the fore-mast square-rigged. These vessels hail mainly from Goole.

Binding-strakes are deep planks between the hatchways. Extra thickness of planking in ships' decks.

Binn.—A place for storing articles and rubbish.

Binnacle.—A stand, or box of brass, or wood in which a compass is placed.

Bird's-nest.—A contrivance at a masthead from which whalemen keep a look-out.

Birthed.—Covered in with boards.

Bittacle.—The ancient name of binnacle.

Bitt-pins.—Iron bars employed to prevent the cable from slipping off the cross-piece of the bitts.

Bitts.—The ends of timbers which project through the decks. They are meant to fasten anything to.

Black Jack.—A name for the black flag flown by pirates.

Black South-Easter cap.—The name given to a canopy of dark cloud upon Table Mountain.

Blackwall lead.—A Blackwall lead is to take a rope under a belaying-pin and swig back on it. See Swig.

Blade.—The flat part of an oar.

Bleed the bags.—Opening bags of grain for filling up all spaces, to prevent shifting.

Bleed the buoy.—To let the water out of a buoy.

Bleed the monkey.—To steal grog from a mess-tub called the monkey. This term is exclusively naval. I have never heard of monkeys in merchant ships.

Blind.—A term applied to rivet-holes in two ship's plates whose holes do not lie fair so as to make one clear orifice when placed together.

Blockading.—Preventing vessels from passing in or out of a harbour in war-time.

Block-model.—A miniature of a ship, a model, constructed in accordance with the specification of the ship to be built.

Blood and entrails.—The Yankee name for the British ensign.

Blow-off cock.—A cock at the bottom of a marine boiler for blowing down the boiler and for letting a portion of the water escape into the sea by the pressure of the steam.

Blow the gaff.—To inform against a man. "He has blown the gaff," he has "split."

Blow-valve.—A valve used for establishing the vacuum necessary to start an engine.

Blubber-boiler.—A name for a whaleman.

Blue Charts.—Charts whose backs are blue, sold by private firms: a term to distinguish them from official or Admiralty charts.

Blue Jacket.—A man-of-war's man. Never applied to merchant seamen.

Blue nose.—A name given to a Nova Scotian.

Blue pigeon.—A name given to the sounding-lead.

Blue Peter.—A blue flag with a white square in the centre, hoisted at the fore to denote that the vessel is about to sail.

Blue shirt at masthead.—A signal to denote that assistance is required.

Bluff.—A term applied to a ship's bows, and means full and square.

Bluff of the bow.—The fullest point of a ship's bow on either side.

Board.—A stretch by sailing on one tack. To make a *long board* is to go on sailing a long distance on one tack. A *short board* is of course the opposite. Also to *board a ship* is to enter her for a hand-to-hand conflict. Also to go on board of her, as "The pilot boarded us at such and such an hour."

Boarding-knife.—A long double-edged sword, mounted on a straight handle, used in the operation of "cutting in" in whalers.

Board of Trade.—A department of the State that undertakes, *inter alia*, the general superintendence of matters relating to merchant ships and seamen, and that is authorized to carry into execution the provisions of the various Merchant Shipping Acts.

Boats.—Ships' boats are variously named. Until recently in the merchant service those boats which hung by davits abaft the main-mast were called *quarter-boats*, the boat over the stern was called the *gig*, and the boat stowed forward was called the *long-boat*. All this is now altered. Boats are stowed on skids, and called first and second lifeboats, first and second cutters, pinnace, &c.

Boat hook.—A pole furnished with an iron hook and spike for shoving off or holding on to an object when in a boat.

Boat iron.—A contemptuous term applied to the iron used by ship-builders on account of its quality.

Boat-steerers.—Men who steer whale-boats when chasing whales. They are a kind of petty officers aboard whalers.

Boatswain.—One of the crew who has charge of the rigging and oversees the men. In the navy he is a warrant officer. In small merchant vessels he used to take the duties of second mate and keep a look-out. When merely boatswain he "sleeps in" all night unless all hands are called. He is a responsible man, a superior seaman, and heads the crew forward.

Bob-line.—A line used for suspending a plummet to point out the centre of certain blocks in a repairing dock.

Bob-stay.—A rope or chain to hold the bowsprit down to its place.

Body-plan.—The name given to a drawing descriptive of the largest vertical athwartship section of a ship.

Body-post.—A piece of timber rising from the keel of a vessel before the stern-post.

Boiler.—The generator and reservoir of the motive power of the steam engine. It is of various forms and construction, according to the place it occupies, the size of the ship, the fuel to be consumed, &c.

Bold.—This word is usually applied to a steep shore or coast that enables a vessel to draw in close.

Bolsters.—Supports for the eyes of the rigging.

Bolt of canvas.—A roll of sail-cloth from thirty-nine to forty yards long.

Bolt-rope.—A rope sewed to the sides of a sail to give it strength.

Bolts.—Bars of iron or copper used in the building of wooden ships. Copper-fastened means fastened with copper bolts.

Bomb-lance.—An iron tube provided with wings and fired from a gun at a whale, in which it explodes.

Bomb-ship.—A vessel armed with mortars and howitzers for throwing shells.

Bond-note.—A list of bonded or warehoused goods presented at the Custom House.

Bonnet.—A piece of canvas attached to the foot of a jib by lacings, and therefore removable.

Booby.—A sea-bird found in the tropics.

Booby-hatch.—A small after-hatch in ships with poops, under the break of the poop, abaft the main hatch. But the name seems now to be given to a hatch in any part of the ship.

Book.—The name given to a number of hides.

Boom-boats.—Boats which are stowed on the spare booms of a ship.

Boom-brace.—A tackle consisting of a whip and pendant fitted to the end of a studding-sail boom.

Boom fore-sail.—A square or fore-and-aft fore-sail, the foot of which is extended by a boom.

Boom-irons.—Iron rings or hoops fitted at the yard-arms for the support of the studding-sail booms.

Boom-jigger.—A tackle used for rigging top-mast studding sail booms in and out.

Boomkin.—An outrigger at the bows, to which the fore-tack is brought.

Boom main-sail.—A fore-and-aft sail on the main-mast, whose foot is extended by a boom.

Booms.—Spare spars, top-masts, &c., stowed on deck.

Boom-sheets.—Ropes for steadying the spanker-boom and for adjusting it to the angle required by the sail.

Bora.—A furious wind encountered in the Gulf of Venice.

Bore.—The rushing up of water from the rapid rise of a tide when it is very large in proportion to its depth.

Born weak.—Said of a ship feebly built.

Boss.—A large protuberance forged on the inner stern-post of a ship into which the tube of the screw or propeller shaft is secured.

Bottomry is the pledging of a ship, cargo, and freight for money for the purpose of completing a voyage.

Bounty.—A reward offered to merchant seamen to ship in the Royal Navy.

'Bout ship!—Namely, about ship! The order for putting the vessel round on the other tack.

Bow.—To bow the sea, said of a ship as she pitches or meets the sea when almost head to wind.

Bower.—A working anchor; there are two. See Best bower.

Bow-grace.—A rope fender or protection used over the bows of a vessel to prevent the ice from injuring them.

Bowline-bridle.—Ropes spliced into cringles on the leech of a sail to which the bowline is toggled.

Bowline-knot.—The end of a rope laid over the standing part in such a way as to form a fixed bight. Other bowline-knots are, a *running bowline*, a *bowline* *on a bight*, and a *bowline-bend*. These and other knots cannot be taught by written explanations.

Bowlines.—Ropes attached to bridles or loops in the leech or side of a sail for dragging it forward to catch the wind when the yards are braced up.

Bowls.—A kind of small kegs for buoying nets.

Bowman.—The headmost rower in a boat.

Bow-port.—A hole cut in the bow of a ship for loading and discharging timber.

Bowse.—To pull. *Bowse taut!* signifies haul taut.

Bowse up the jib.—Said of a man who drinks in order to get drunk.

Bowsprit.—A large spar projecting over the bows. In ships another spar is fixed on the bowsprit, called the jib boom and flying-jib boom. Formerly the flying-jib boom was a separate spar and could be rigged in and out like a studding-sail boom; but it is now of one piece with the jib boom, like a top-gallant and royal-mast.

Bowsprit-shrouds.—Ropes to support the bowsprit sideways, answering to the bowsprit as the shrouds do to the masts.

Box (to).—To put fish into trunks or boxes.

Box-hauling.—Wearing a vessel in a narrow circumference by running her up into the wind and backing the fore-yards.

Boxing.—The name given to a practice among smacks belonging to the N. and N.E. coast, of sending fish in boats to the steam-cutters for conveyance home.

Boxing the compass.—Reciting the points of the compass all round.

Boxing-trim.—A term applied to a ship ready to fight.

Box-kelson.—A kelson formed of plates and angle irons across the top of the flooring to which it is fixed.

Box-keys.—Implements for turning the nuts of large bolts.

Box off.—To turn a ship's head from the wind by backing a head-sail.

Box-ventilator system.—A mode of ventilating the hold of a ship by means of tunnels, about eight inches deep, running fore and aft through the cargo, midway between the shifting boards and the sides of the ship; the sides of the tunnels being formed by boards held together by pieces of wood, and the ends terminating in open spaces or in shafts.

Boy.—An apprentice. Lads who formerly made a regular portion of a ship's company. It is a term of contempt for a green hand. Therefore a "boy" may be a man.

Braces.—Ropes attached to square yards to haul them round so as to adapt the sails to the direction of the wind. They take their name from the sails or yards which they govern; as the fore-topgallant braces, the main-topsail braces, the crossjack braces, the mizzen-royal braces, &c. Also the eyes by which a rudder hangs. See Gudgeons.

Bracket or longitudinal system.—A method of iron ship building in which the floor-plates are carried to the top of the double-bottom space, making that the floor for tonnage measurement.

Brails.—Ropes attached to the leech of a spanker or try-sail for taking it in. Hence you *brail up* a gaff-sail, and *clew up* a square sail.

Brake.—The handle of an old-fashioned ship's pump.

Brass-bound and copper-fastened.—Said of a lad dressed in a midshipman's uniform.

Brass-bounder.—A midshipman.

Brass-work.—All the brass on a ship's decks, such as the rails, binnacle hood, &c.

Breaching.—A whale is said to *breach* when it rises with such velocity out of the water as to project three-fourths of its length in the air, and then in falling creates a mass of white water.

Bread-barge.—A tray for holding ship's biscuit for immediate consumption.

Breadth-moulded.—The greatest extreme breadth over the frames or ribs of a ship, but *inside* the plates or planking.

Break.—The forward termination of the poop called "the break of the poop" and the after termination of the forecastle.

Break-beams.—Pieces of timber introduced where planking terminates.

Breaker.—A small water-cask for a boat.

Break off.—A ship is said to *break off* when the wind draws ahead and forces her out of her course, or from the direction towards which she was heading at the time.

Breaming.—Cleaning a vessel's bottom by burning.

Breast backstays.—Supports for a mast from the head of it to the chains.

Breast-hooks.—These are arms of timber or iron to unite the two sides of a ship's bows.

Breast-rope.—The name of a rope over a ship's side for a man to lean against when using the lead.

Breast-shores.—Timbers used for supporting a ship in a repairing-dock.

Breech.—The angle of a knee-timber.

Breeching.—A rope to restrain the recoil of a gun when discharged.

Breeching-rings.—Rings in a ship's side to make the breechings of a gun fast to.

Breech-sight.—A notch on a cannon to enable the gunner to aim the projectile.

Breeze.—Any kind of wind short of a gale, characterized by adjectives, such as strong breeze, fresh breeze, moderate breeze, light breeze, &c. Sailors usually say "a breeze of wind."

Breezing up.—Said of wind gradually freshening.

Bricklayer's clerk.—One of the hundred names given to a lubberly sailor.

Brick-system.—In iron ship building, a method that brings each butt at the middle of those plates which are just above and below it.

Bridge of the furnace.—The brickwork at the back of the furnace in a steamer.

Bridle-port.—A square port in a ship's bows for guns or mooring bridles.

Bridles.—Fore and after bridles are ropes connected with the trawls used by smacks.

Brig.—A square-rigged vessel with two masts, tops, and crosstrees. She is in all respects rigged like two masts of a full-rigged ship.

Brigantine.—A two-masted vessel. Her fore-mast is rigged like a brig's; her main-mast like a schooner's. She carries a square top-sail and topgallant sail.

Bright light.—A white or yellowish light, to distinguish it from green or red. "She carried a bright light at the mast-head," that is, a lantern of uncoloured glass.

Brine cock.—A cock attached to marine boilers for blowing off as much salt as is contained in the water that is blown off.

Bring up.—A vessel brings up when she drops her anchor.

Broach.—To open. To break in upon, as broaching cargo.

Broaching cargo.—Stealing from cargo whilst at sea or in harbour.

Broaching to.—When a ship's head in running is swept round towards the wind.

Broad pennant.—A swallow-tailed flag flown by a commodore.

Broadside.—The whole side of a ship. Also said when the guns on a vessel's side are discharged simultaneously or very rapidly one after another.

Broken water.—Agitated water among shoals or sunken rocks.

Brought by the lee.—This is the situation of a vessel when, whilst running, the wind chops from one quarter to the other of her.

Brought to.—A vessel is brought to when stopped after being chased.

Bucket-rack.—A shelf with holes in it, in which buckets used for washing down the decks are kept.

Bucklar.—The lower part of a port-lid.

Bugle-man.—A person who formerly sounded a horn as a signal for sailors to board a ship.

Bulkhead.—Partitions to divide a cabin or hold, or to keep water from flowing beyond a certain space.

Bull.—A small keg.

Bullies.—A term of encouragement, if not of endearment, as "Tail on here, bullies!" "We're the bully lads!" &c.

Bulljine.—Sailor's name for a locomotive engine; borrowed, like a good deal more, from the Americans.

Bullock-blocks.—Blocks under the trestle-trees, through which the top-sail ties are rove.

Bull-rope.—A hawser rove through a block on the bowsprit and attached to a buoy to keep it clear of the ship.

Bull's eye.—A wooden thimble without a sheave. Also a piece of thick glass let into the deck over a cabin.

Bull's-eye squall.—A squall that comes in a clear sky and fine weather and shows like a bright white spot at or near the zenith.

Bully for you!-A kind of congratulatory address among sailors of a meaning impossible to define exactly.

Bulwarks.—The protection around a vessel, consisting of solid planking fixed to stanchions.

Bumboat.—A boat that comes off to ships to sell provisions, fruit, &c.

Bumpers.—The name of wooden fenders slung over a ship's side when among the ice.

Bumpkin.—A small spar or out-rigger in the stern of a yawl. Also a timber on either quarter of a ship for the main-brace blocks.

Bumpkin-shrouds.—Small ropes for supporting a yawl's bumpkin or out-rigger.

Bundle up!—A cry to sailors to come up! Jump up!

Bunk.—A shelf in a cabin or forecastle on which a sailor or passenger sleeps.

Bunker.—A space near the engine-room in a steamer where coals for consumption in the furnaces are kept.

Bunt.—The middle of a square-sail.

Bunting.—Stuff of which flags are made.

Bunt-jigger.—A tackle used in furling a whole top-sail.

Buntlines.—Ropes secured to the poop of a square-sail to haul that part of it up to the yard.

Buntline spans.—Pieces of rope with a cringle for the buntlines to reeve through.

Buntline-toggles.—Toggles strapped round the foot-rope of a sail for fitting the buntlines.

Bunt-whip.—A rope used in furling a course.

Buoys are of two kinds: one to denote danger and to serve as a guide to keep ships clear of shoals, rocks, wrecks, &c.; the other, styled anchor-buoys, are used to show the position of the anchor, that the cable may be prevented from fouling it when a ship is riding in a tide-way or changeable current. It is also of use to enable a master to recover his anchor when the cable is slipped or broken in a gale of wind.

Burden.—A ship's burden is the weight in tons she can carry.

Burgee.—A flag with a name or sign upon it, to denote the service, club, &c, the vessel that flies it belongs to.

Burgoo.—Porridge. It is the sailor's name for it.

Burton-pendants.—Ropes which hang down on each side of a top-mast for setting up the top-mast rigging, &c.

Bush.—A lining of metal to diminish friction.

Busses.—Dutch fishing-vessels.

Butter-box.—A lumpish, uncouth vessel. "She has the run of a butter-box."

Butterfly.—A barge.

Butter-rig.—A butter-rigged schooner is a top-sail schooner whose topgallant yard when lowered comes down on the top-sail yard and stows there.

Buttock.—A plank under the lower counter rail on the stern of a ship.

Buttock rules.—Metal fittings beneath the counter of wooden screw-steamers, connecting the two stern-posts.

Butts.—The ends of planks or iron or steel plates where they meet.

Butt-straps.—Iron plates fitted behind the butt-ends of plates on an iron ship.

By the board.—Overboard; over the ship's side. "Her masts went by the board."

By the head.—Said of a vessel when she is deeper, when afloat, in the fore than in the after part.

By the wind.—A sailor's expression when he is "hard up." Also said of a ship close hauled on a wind.

C

Cabin.—A room in a ship for sleeping and eating in. Berth is perhaps the correct name for a sleeping-compartment, as by cabin is generally understood the place where the meals are taken.

Cable.—A chain or rope to anchor by, 150 fathoms long. There are 12 lengths in a chain, every length being 12½ fathoms.

Cable-laid.—A rope composed of nine strands, and made by forming three ropes of three strands each, laid from right to left, and then laying the three ropes into one from left to right, is called cable-laid.

Cable's length.—One hundred fathoms.

Cable-tier.—A place in a ship where the cables are stowed.

Caboose.—An old name for the galley of a merchantman.

Cade.—A barrel of herrings.

Caissoon.—A floating gate to close the entrance of a dock.

Calavances.—Small beans used for soup instead of peas.

Calibre.—The capacity of the bore of a gun.

Calling of the sea.—A peculiar moaning sound heard on the coast, and interpreted to signify approaching bad weather.

Cam.—A metal disk, graduated, and used for giving the proper motion to the expansion valve of a marine engine.

Camber.—The name given in ship-building to a rise in a vessel's deck in the centre of it.

Camel.—The name of a contrivance for helping a ship over a bar or shoal.

Camfer.—To remove the edge of a timber.

Can-hooks.—A chain with hooks for slinging a cask by the chimes.

Cannon-petro.—A piece of ordnance formerly used in ships; it threw about a 24 lb. shot.

Canopy.—An awning used in boats.

Cant purchase.—A tackle for turning a dead whale over, for flensing or flaying it.

Cantle-piece.—A batten, used in the building of certain kinds of smacks, placed above the platform to prevent it from rising.

Cantline.—A girtline. (See this word.)

Cant-timbers.—The timber in the extreme end of a ship, which is rounded off.

Canvas covers.—Covers for enclosing fore-and-aft sails when furled, extending from the end of the gaff to the tack-cringle of the spanker and try-sails, and for jibs the length of the foot of those sails.

Cap.—A piece of wood or iron that fits over the head of a mast or bowsprit to support the spar above or beyond, as a top-mast or a jib boom.

Capacity.—A ship's burden.

Cape Cod-man.—A man who belongs to any part of the coast of Massachusetts south of Boston.

Cap of the block.—The upper piece of the tiers of blocks on which the keel of a wooden ship is laid.

Cap-scuttles.—Apertures in the deck with raised coamings.

Capsize.—To upset.

Capstan.—A barrel of wood or iron revolved by bars.

Capstan-bars.—Long pieces of wood made to fit the holes in the capstan, and used when weighing anchor, transporting ship, &c.

Captain.—A naval officer. Strictly speaking, he is the officer in command of a line-of-battle ship, or a frigate mounting 20 guns. Only naval officers of that rank have the right to style themselves captain, though it is nowadays assumed by even the skipper of a collier.

Caravel.—An old type of vessel with an undecked centre, high bow and stern, and a forecastle and cabin for the crew.

Cardinal.—The cardinal points of a compass are North, South, East, and West.

Careen.—To heave a vessel down by tackles at the mast-heads; or she may be careened by shifting weights to one side: a method of doing it that caused the loss of the *Royal George*.

Carlings.—Short pieces of timber between the beams of a ship.

Carrick-bend.—A bend for joining two large ropes by loops which jam the ends.

Carronade.—A short gun, so-called because it was invented in 1779 at Carron in Scotland.

Carry.—To carry a ship is to seize her by boarding.

Carry away.—To break. To carry away a mast is to lose it by its breaking off.

Carvel.—A small lateen-rigged vessel.

Carvel-built.—A term signifying the planking of a vessel laid smooth and the seams caulked.

Case.—A whaleman's term for the upper part of the head of a whale.

Case or Canister.—A shot consisting of a number of small iron balls packed in a tin case that fits the gun from which it is fired.

Cashier.—To dismiss from the Royal Navy by court-martial.

Casing-cover.—A place in the marine engine for the slide-valve rod to pass through.

Castaway.—A mariner shipwrecked on a desert place. Also, to wilfully wreck a ship.

Casting.—The moving of the ship's head away from the anchor after weighing.

Cast of the lead.—Plumbing the water with the lead to sound for the bottom.

Cat.—The tackle used for hoisting the anchor to the cat-head, sometimes called the cat-tackle. Also the cat-o'-nine-tails.

Cataract.—An arrangement, consisting of a brass cylinder filled with oil or water, for checking the fall of the expansion valves of marine engines when made upon the Cornish principle.

Cat-back.—A small line bent on to the cat-hook to turn the hook as required.

Cat-block.—A large block forming a portion of the cat-tackle.

Catch a crab.—To miss striking the water with your oar when rowing, the usual result of which is that you fall heels over head backwards.

Cat-chain.—A length of small chain to enable an anchor to be hove high enough to hook the catfall in vessels built with ram bows.

Catch-ratline.—Every fifth ratline is so called, because it is distinguished from the others by being seized to the after-shroud.

Cat harpens, or cat-harpings, were ropes formerly used under the tops for bracing in the shrouds.

Cat-head.—A large piece of timber that projects over the bows of a ship on each side for the anchor to hang to.

Cat-holes.—Places in a vessel's quarters for springs or warps to lead through.

Cat-rig.—A fore-and-aft sail set with a gaff and boom that stretches very nearly the whole length of the boat.

Catspaw.—A light passage of air that ruffles the water. Also a knot for slinging by a hook.

Catted.—Cat-headed. Said of the anchor when it has been hoisted to the cat-head.

Cattle-pens.—Stalls or boxes in which horned cattle are carried at sea. The cattle are ranged in two rows, one on each side the ship, each beast having a separate head-rope, which is passed with a bight round one of the horns, and a half-hitch round the other, and then secured.

Caulk.—To drive oakum into the seams of planks.

Caulker.—A heavy dose of rum. Also, a lie.

Caulking.—An iron ship is caulked by a man holding against the edge of a plate a chisel or caulking-tool, which is struck with a hammer, thus filling up the crevices between the plates.

Caulking-irons.—Sharp iron wedges for driving oakum into the seams.

Ceiling.—The inside planking of a vessel.

Central track.—The line upon which the centre of a revolving storm moves.

Centre-burton.—A tackle sometimes used for sending a top-sail aloft.

Certificate of competency.—A certificate granted to persons who have passed the requisite examination for master, chief mate, only mate, or second mate.

Certificate of registry.—A form giving the name of a ship, her construction, measurements, tonnage, &c., signed by a registrar.

Certificate of service.—A certificate to entitle an officer who has served in a British foreign-going ship before January, 1851, or in a home-trade passenger-ship before 1854, to serve in the capacity he formerly filled.

Chafe.—Wear and tear.

Chafing-gear.—Mats, canvas, small stuff, battens, &c., affixed to the foot of sails, to backstays, &c., to prevent them from being rubbed through.

Chain-hooks.—Hooks used for dragging the cable along the deck.

Chain-pipes.—Orifices through which the cables lead out of the chain-lockers on to the deck.

Chain-plates.—Iron bars fitted to the sides to which the lower dead-eyes are affixed.

Chain-pump.—A pump formed of buckets working on an endless chain and operated on by a wheel and handle.

Chalk for watches.—A method among crews of settling their turns at the anchor watch by making marks in divisions of a circle and then having them rubbed out.

Channels.—Platforms over the side nearly abreast of each mast, to which shrouds and backstays are set up.

Channel-rail.—A piece of moulding for finishing off the front of a channel.

Chantey.—A song, a chorus.

Chapelling.—A name given to a manoeuvre by which a ship is wore without bracing the head-yards.

Charter-party.—A contract in writing for the letting of the whole or part of a vessel for freight.

Chart-house.—An iron or wooden deck structure on a steamer, for the convenience of consulting the charts.

Chase.—A pursued ship is called the chase.

Chase-guns.—The guns in the chase-ports.

Chase-port.—A port on each side amidships of a vessel to enable a gun to be fired forward.

Chasse-marée.—A French three-masted lugger for protecting the fisheries, &c.

Check.—To check a brace is to slack or ease it off a little.

Check-rope.—A rope made fast to anything stationary, for the purpose of bringing a moving vessel to a stand.

Chequered sides.—Said of a ship with ports painted on a white ground.

Cheeks.—Side pieces on a mast for the trestle-trees to rest on.

Cheeks, the marine.—An imaginary being in a man-of-war.

Chew of tobacco.—A quid. Also called a *chaw*.

Chilled-shot.—Cast-iron shot tempered to great hardness by being rapidly cooled.

Chimes.—The projected ends of the staves of a cask.

Chinse.— Caulking with a small iron.

Chips.—Sailor's name for ship's carpenter.

Chock-ablock.—Said when anything hauled by a rope through a block is brought hard up against the block.

Chocks.—Wooden supports for the bottom of a boat to rest on.

Chock up.—Said of anything hoisted when it is as high as it will go.

Chowder.—A mess of codfish, biscuit, &c.

Chow-dow.—Eatables.

Chronometer.—A timepiece to indicate Greenwich mean time for the purpose of finding the longitude.

Circles of longitude.—Great circles passing through the poles of the ecliptic and cutting it at right angles.

Circular friction-break.—An excellent suggestion to provide against the breaking of steerage-gear. A notched band of iron encircles the rudder-head at the deck, and the rudder-head is furnished with a tiller or break-handle. If the rudder-gear gives way, a man presses the break-handle down into the notched band of iron, and so stops the rudder at any required position.

Circular stern.—A stern furnished with stern timbers which heel upon the fashion timber, and extend round the stern from side to side.

Civil day.—A day that begins at midnight and ends on the next midnight.

Clack-valve.—A flat valve with a hinge joint.

Clamps.—The inside planking immediately under the shelf of each deck.

Clamp-screw.—A screw in the back of the index of a sextant used for fixing the index to the arc.

Clapper.—The valve of a pump-box.

Clasp-hooks.—Two hooks working on one pivot.

Classification clubs.—Clubs for insuring vessels.

Claw-off.—To ratch off a lee shore.

Clean swept.—A ship with all the ballast out.

Cleanser-boat.—A mud-hopper. See Hoppers.

Clearance.—Papers presented by a shipmaster comprising his victualling bill, receipts for light dues, &c. Also the name given to the space between the piston and the cylinder bottom in a marine engine, at the end of a stroke.

Clear side.—The height from the water to the upper side of the plank of the deck from which the depth of the hold is measured.

Cleat.—A piece of wood to make the running gear, sheets, &c., fast to.

Clew.—The corner of a square sail. The after corner of a fore-and-aft sail.

Clew-garnets.—Ropes attached to the clews of a course for hauling it up.

Clewing down.—Hauling upon the clew-lines without starting the sheets, so as to bring the yard down. Done in reefing.

Clew-jiggers.—Tackles for clewing up a top-sail. They lead over the forward side of a sail.

Clew-lines.—Ropes attached to the lower corners of square sails for hauling them up to the middle of the yard.

Clinch.—A half-hitch stopped to its own part.

Clinker, or clincher-built.—A vessel so built that the bottom edge of every plank overlays the next below it.

Clinker-bar.—A bar fixed across the top of the ash-pit.

Clinkers.—Matter not consumable by fire left on the fire-bars.

Clipper.—A sharp, fine-lined vessel: a fast sailer.

Close-hauled.—Said of a ship when lying close to the wind.

Close-port.—A port up a river.

Cloth.—A strip of canvas. See Bolt of canvas.

Cloud-cleaner.—An imaginary sail jokingly assumed to be carried by Yankee ships.

Clove-hitch.—The end of a rope passed over anything and brought up under and around behind its standing part and up through its own part.

Clubbing.—Drifting with the anchor over.

Club-haul.—A method of tacking when on a lee shore by getting a spring on the lee anchor and leading the spring to the lee quarter, then putting the helm down, and when the ship loses way, letting go the anchor, hauling round the main-yards and cutting the spring when the sails are full on the other tack.

Clump-block.—A short, thick block of extra strength.

Clumsy-cleet.—A knee-brace in the bow of a whale-boat.

Coach-whip.—The pennant flown by a man-of-war.

Coalman.—A name for a collier.

Coamings.—Pieces of raised wood or iron to prevent water from rolling down the hatchways.

Coaning.—A method of uniting small pieces of timber.

Coaster.—A term applied to a vessel that trades between or among ports situated in the United Kingdom.

Coasting-chart.—A chart constructed on the presumption that small portions of the earth's surface are planes.

Cob.—To beat a man with a piece of flat wood.

Coble.—A north country fishing or pilot boat.

Cock-bill.—The situation of an anchor when it hangs at the cathead.

Cocket.—A card affixed to a victualling-bill, and serving as a shipmaster's customs-warrant for sailing.

Cockpit.—A place under the lower gun-deck of a man-of-war, made one of the most familiar of sea names by Captain Marryatt's novels.

Cod.—To cod a man is to gull him.

Code pennant.—A flag hoisted to denote that the particular code of signals called the Commercial Code is used.

Codline.—An 18-thread line.

Coil.—To bring a rope into a small compass by forming it into rings, one lying on another. Also, to lay a rope over a belaying-pin in fakes.

Coir rope.—A rope made of cocoa-nut fibres.

Cold-chisel.—A chisel tempered for cutting cold iron.

Collar.—An eye in the end of standing rigging to go over the masthead.

Collier.—A vessel that carries coals.

Collier's purchase.—Hooking the cat-block to a strop on the cable, and clapping on the fish-purchase to the fall.

Colours.—The ensign of the country to which a ship belongs and which she hoists.

Colt.—A piece of knotted rope for beating a man.

Column.—A number of men-of-war in a group.

Column of division.—Divisions of a fleet.

Combers.—Large seas or breakers.

Combing sea.—A large arching wave.

Combustion-chamber.—A place situated at the end of a furnace, through which the gases and flames pass before entering the tubes.

Come home.—An anchor when it does not hold in warping, is said to come home.

Come to.—To round into the wind.

Come up.—To ease up a rope; to slacken it off.

Commander of a column.—The senior officer of the column.

Commodore.—The senior officer in command of a detached squadron.

Common steam.—Steam in contact with the water that produced it.

Companion.—A wooden hood over a hatch.

Companion-ladder.—Steps leading down the companion-hatch to the cabin.

Compass-card.—A circle of mica or cardboard divided into thirty-two parts, called points of the compass.

Complain.—Masts and spars are said to complain when they creak during the labouring of the ship.

Complement.—The crew of a ship. The number of working hands necessary for the navigation of a vessel.

Composant.—A name given by sailors to the fiery exhalations which are seen burning at yard-arms and boom-ends in calms and gales of wind at night.

Composite great circle sailing.—When the Great Circle track carries the ship into a higher latitude than is proper, a certain latitude is assumed as the highest the ship should attain, and the shortest route under these conditions is called composite great circle sailing.

Composite ship.—A ship whose frame is composed of iron and covered with timber planking.

Compound engine.—An engine with two cylinders, into the smaller of which the steam enters and works the piston, and then passes into the large cylinder, where it is condensed.

Compressor.—A lever for stopping the chain cable when running out.

Con.—To direct the steering of a vessel.

Concluding-line.—A small rope leading down the middle of a Jacob's ladder.

Condenser gauge.—A tube for indicating the vacuum in the condenser of a marine engine.

Constant of aberration.—Displacement in the sun's longitude.

Constructive total loss.—The term applied to injuries of which the repairs would exceed the value of the ship damaged.

Contract.—A document embodying all the items contained in the various shipping bills.

Convoy.—One or more merchant-vessels sailing under the protection of a war-ship.

Coolie.—An Indian or Chinese labourer.

Cooper.—A person who repairs casks, &c., on board a ship.

Coopering.—The name given to a fraudulent traffic among North-Sea smacksmen, who barter the fish belonging to their owners for tobacco and spirits sold by vessels which hang about those waters and whose people are called "coopers."

Copper-bottomed.—Said of a ship whose bottom is sheathed with copper.

Copper-fastened.—Said of a wooden ship whose frames are secured to one another by copper bolts.

Coppers.—The boilers in the galley for cooking.

Cordage.—A landsman's term for the rigging of a ship. Tackling is another shore word for the same thing.

Corner chock.—Removable pieces of wood to enable the wood-ends to be caulked without disturbing the hawse-pipes.

Corvette.—A flush decked ship with one tier of guns. Formerly she was sometimes furnished with a poop or round-house, and a top-gallant forecastle.

Cot.—A swinging bed formed of a frame covered with canvas.

Counter.—The hinder portion of a vessel forming a portion of her stern.

Counter.—An instrument fitted with wheelwork and an index hand, which hand is moved forward a certain distance in correspondence with every stroke of the engine. It is used to show speed, allowance being made for "slip."

Counter-brace.—Heaving to.

Counter-bracing.—Working the sails so as to make a ship range ahead or stop at will.

Country-wallah.—An East Indian native ship.

Course.—The direction to be steered by a ship.

Courses.—The lowest sails of a square-rigged vessel.

Court-martial.—A court composed of five, but not exceeding nine, members, for trying naval officers and seamen charged with wrong-doing.

Court of Survey.—A court composed of a judge and two assessors for deciding cases of the detention of ships.

Cove-rail.—A moulding on the stern of a ship for decoration.

Cowl.—The deck or top part of a ventilator for ventilating holds, engine-rooms, cabins, &c.

Coxswain.—One who steers a boat and has charge of her.

Crab-windlass.—A light windlass.

Cracking on.—To pile on sail in a strong wind.

Crack ship.—A first-class vessel for discipline, sailing, &c.

Cradle.—A fabric set to the bottom of a ship about to be launched.

Craft.—Any kind of vessel.

Cranage.—Payment for the use of cranes.

Crane.—A machine worked by hand or steam for loading and unloading vessels.

Crane-barge.—A barge fitted with a crane.

Crane-lines.—Small ropes used for keeping the backstays clear of the yards when braced sharp up.

Crank.—Want of stability. A ship that leans sharply under small canvas. Also, an iron handle for pumps.

Crank-hatches.—Protections on deck for the engine-cranks.

Crank-pin.—The pin to which the connecting-rod of a marine engine is attached.

Crazy.—A crazy ship is an old, rotten ship.

Creeper.—A kind of grapnel.

Crew.—All the officers and men who man a vessel.

Crib.—A small sleeping-berth.

Crimp.—A man who was formerly allowed to collect crews for ships. A plunderer of seamen. A lodging or boarding-house keeper for sailors.

Cringle.—A strand of rope, like an eye, confining an iron ring, worked into the bolt-rope.

Crinkum-crankum whales.—Whales which, according to the whalemen, "can't be cotched."

Cripple.—To disable a ship by firing at her.

Croaky.—A curved plank.

Cross.—To cross a yard is to send it aloft, fit the rigging, and leave it square or across.

Cross-bars.—Round bars of iron used as levers.

Cross-jack.—Pronounced cro'-jack. The lowest square-sail on a ship's mizzen-mast.

Cross-jack yard.—The lowest yard on a ship's mizzen-mast.

Cross-pauls.—Long pieces of plank marked with the breadth of a ship at various stations, and secured to the timbers to preserve the form of the vessel whilst she remains in frame.

Cross-piece.—A timber connecting two bitts.

Cross-sea.—A confused, heavy sea that follows a circular storm. Waves moving in different directions. "Chopping sea" is perhaps another term for the same thing.

Cross-spales.—Timbers to keep the sides of a vessel together until the knees are bolted.

Cross-staff.—An instrument anciently used for measuring altitudes at sea.

Cross-trees.—Cross-pieces of timber on top of the trestle-trees.

Crotch.—A notched stick of a peculiar form, fixed in the starboard gunwale of a whaling-boat near the bow as a rest for the wooden extremity of the harpoon.

Crotch the boom.—To steady the boom of a spanker or gaff main-sail by resting it in the crutch or crotch.

Crowd.—To **crowd sail** is to set all sail. To **crowd a vessel off** is to claw off the land under a heavy press of canvas.

Crowfoot.—A number of small cords spreading out from a kind of block, and used to suspend an awning.

Crown.—That part of an anchor where the shank and arms meet.

Crown of aberration.—A spurious circle round the true circle of the sun.

Cruise.—Strictly, traversing a given part of the ocean on the lookout for an enemy. But a trip in a yacht or steamer that extends over a few days is now called a cruise.

Cruiser.—A man-of-war employed for the protection of merchant-men in the Channel and around the coast.

Crupper.—A ring-bolt for the train-tackle of a gun-carriage.

Crupper chain.—A chain passed round the bowsprit and the heel of the jib boom.

Crutch.—A fork to steady a boom when the sail is furled. See Crotch the boom.

Crutches.—Plates used in iron ships where the space becomes too narrow for beams and stringers. Also timbers or iron arms to unite the sides of a ship abaft.

Cubbridge heads.—Bulkheads formerly fortified with guns for firing along the decks in order to sweep them.

Cuckold's neck.—A knot to secure a rope to a spar.

Cuddy.—The saloon under the poop.

Cuddy jig.—The sprawling about of landsmen at sea on a heaving deck.

Cuddy-legs.—Large herrings.

Culvert.—A large drain to let out the water from a wet dock as the tide falls.

Cuntline.—The space between the bilges of casks stowed side by side.

Curios.—Curiosities. Objects collected by sailors in distant countries.

Current.—A body of water which, being in motion, carries all floating bodies with it.

Current-sailing.—A method of determining the true course and distance of a ship when in a current.

Cushee-piece.—A gun invented by Sir John Leake, in 1677. It was intended as a bow gun, and discharged shells and what were called "carcasses."

Cut and run.—Literally this was only possible when cables were of hemp and could be cut. It is now meant to slip in a gale of wind.

Cut of his jib.—A man's appearance. "I don't like the cut of his jib," said in reference to the appearance of a surly-looking man.

Cut out.—To cut out a ship is to carry her by boats when under a fort and remove her.

Cut-splice.—This is formed by cutting a rope in two and splicing each to the standing part of the other so as to make an oblong eye.

Cutter.—A ship's boat. Also, a one-masted vessel fitted with a bowsprit to run in and out and a jib that sets flying.

Cutter-brig.—A square-rigged vessel with a fore-and-aft main-sail. She has two masts, the after one a jigger-mast.

Cutter stay fashion.—This is said of a dead-eye turned in with the end of the shroud down.

Cutting down.—Passing a knife over the laniards of a hammock so as to let the occupant fall on deck.

Cutting in.—The dissection of a whale alongside a whaler, and the twisting of "the blanket" into the blubber-room fall under this name.

Cyclone.—A revolving tempest of wind.

Cylinder-cover.—A lid through which the piston-rod of a marine engine works.

Cylinder-jacket.—A casing to the cylinder of an engine to prevent the outer air from cooling the steam in the cylinder.

D

Dagger.—A timber that forms a portion of the bilge ways of a wooden ship.

Dahabeyah.—A boat used on the river Nile with an arched keel, and fitted with lateen sails.

Damper.—A contrivance for regulating the furnace of a marine boiler by increasing or diminishing the draught.

Dandy.—A vessel rigged like a yawl (see Yawl), but differing from a yawl by having a jib-headed mizzen and no boom to the main-sail.

Dandy funk.—A mess made of powdered biscuit, molasses, and slush.

Dandy wink.—A sort of winch used in smacks for heaving the trawl alongside.

Darbies.—Handcuffs.

Davis's quadrant.—An instrument anciently used for measuring altitudes at sea.

Davits.—Curved iron bars affixed to a ship's sides, by which her boats are suspended.

Davy Jones.—The sailor's devil.

Davy Jones's locker.—The sea, at the bottom of which Davy Jones dwells.

Davy putting on the coppers for the parsons.—Jack's description of the noise made by an approaching storm.

Day's work.—A term given to the computation made from the various courses, corrected, and their corresponding distances.

D-block.—A piece of timber at a ship's side in the channels.

D-thimble.—A thimble lashed to the middle of a yard for attaching the slings.

Dead cargo.—A cargo that makes the ship sluggish or lifeless in a seaway, such as grain.

Dead-doors.—Doors outside those of a quarter gallery.

Deaden.— To impede a ship's progress through the water.

Dead-eyes.—Circular pieces of perforated wood used for the laniards of shrouds.

Dead-eyes under.—Said when a ship is hove down by the force of the wind or by shifting cargo until the dead-eyes of the shrouds and backstays are under water.

Dead fires.—Fires which burn dully or slowly.

Dead-head.—A lump of timber for buoying an anchor.

Dead in steering.—Said of a vessel very slow in answering her helm, most often in consequence of water being in her.

Dead-lights.—Shutters or coverings in open ports.

Dead-men.—Ends of gaskets or reef-points which are left exposed when the sail is furled.

Dead pay.—A term used in the navy to signify unclaimed money.

Dead-plate.—An iron plate fitted to a furnace, for coking bituminous coal before it is thrown into the fire.

Dead-reckoning.—Computing a ship's position by the distance run as shown by the log, having regard to the courses steered, the leeway made, &c. A ship's progress is reckoned in this manner when the weather is thick and no observations can be had.

Dead-rising.—The floor-timbers terminating upon the lower futtock.

Deadsheave.—An aperture in the heel of a top-mast for a second fish-tackle pendant.

Dead slow.—Said of engines revolving at the very slowest pace they can be made to work at.

Dead-wood.—Blocks of timber at each end of the keel.

Dead-works.—A term used to denote all the portion of a loaded ship above water.

Debark.—Landing from a ship.

Deck.—The planked flooring supported by the beams. See Quarter-deck, Forecastle, Poop, &c.

Deck-boy.—A smack apprentice.

Deck-hand.—One of the crew of a fishing-smack.

Deck-house.—A structure on the deck of a ship, in which the crew sleep and live.

Deck-line.—Marks upon a ship's side to indicate the position of her decks. These marks are required by the law to be kept fixed.

Deck-load.—Goods or live stock stowed on the top deck of a vessel.

Deck-sheet.—A studding-sail sheet leading down on deck.

Deck-tackle.—A tackle to assist in weighing the anchor.

Declination.—The declination of an object is an arch of meridian contained between the equinoctial and the centre of the object. It is north or south according as the object is north or south of the equinoctial.

Deep.—The ocean.

Deepening.—Quitting shallow for deeper water, sounding with the lead as you go.

Deep-sea lead.—A lead of from 28 lbs. to 30 lbs. in weight, used for deep soundings.

Deep-waisted.—Applied to a ship whose deck between the poop and topgallant forecastle is deep.

Delivery valve.—In a marine engine, a valve at the top of the air-pump near the hot-well to prevent the return of injected water.

Demand signals.—Flags hoisted as a request for attention.

Demi-cannon.—An old piece of ordnance used in ships. It threw about a 32 lb. shot.

Demijean.—A large bottle containing about five gallons, formerly used for storing rum, &c., on board ship.

Demurrage.—A stipulated sum to be paid by a charterer for delaying a ship after the expiry of the specified lay days.

Departure.—A point from which a ship begins her dead reckoning. Also the east or west distance a ship has made from the meridian of the place she departed from.

Derelict.—A vessel abandoned at sea.

Derrick.—A spar for hoisting weights.

Deviation.—A departure from the ordinary and usual course of a voyage. If without justification, it is taken, should disaster follow, as a discharge of the underwriter's liability.

Deviation of the compass.—The effect produced on the compass by local causes.

Dhow.—An Arab vessel of about 200 tons, lateen-rigged

Dicky.—A term for a second mate.

Difference of latitude.—An arch of a meridian contained between two parallels.

Difference of longitude.—An arch of the equator intercepted between the meridians of two places.

Dinge.—Said of iron plates bent inwards by external pressure.

Dinghey.—A small Indian boat. Also a ship's boat.

Dip.—The angle contained between the sensible and apparent horizons, the angular point being the eye of the observer.

Dip of the needle.—The deflection of one end of the compass needle below the horizon as either pole is approached.

Dip of the wheels.—Said of the depth of water over the top of the vertical board of a paddle-wheel.

Dipper.—A long tin cup for dropping through the bunghole of a cask of fresh water to drink from.

Dipping.—Dipping a sail is lowering it on one and then hoisting it on the other side of the mast.

Direct-acting engine.—An engine in which a rotary motion is obtained by a rod from the head of the piston to the crank acting without side levers.

Discharge.—To unload cargo. A certificate of discharge is a document that states the name of the seaman, the ship he has left, and other particulars.

Disengaging apparatus.—An apparatus for lowering boats by means of self-releasing hooks and other arrangements. There are various contrivances of this kind.

Dish.—To **dish** a sea is to ship a mass of green water over the head or side by a heavy pitch or roll.

Dismantle.—A ship is said to be dismantled when her masts and rigging have been knocked to pieces by shot.

Dismantling shot.—Shot used by the Americans in the war with Great Britain in 1812. It consisted of star shot, double-headed shot, chain shot, and other projectiles, which flow open and cut through the rigging.

Displacement.—The amount of water displaced by the immersion of a ship.

Distance.—The number of miles that a ship has sailed on a direct course in a given time.

Distant signals.—Signals consisting of black balls, pennants, and square flags.

Ditty-bag.—A bag used by seamen for holding small things useful to them.

Dockage.—Charges on vessels using floating docks.

Dockyard maties.—Dockyard artificers.

Doctor.—Sailor's name for a ship's cook.

Dog.—A cross-bar to secure the door of a man-hole for cleaning out a boiler. Also an iron bar used as a purchase. One end is placed against the thing to be lifted, and a tackle is hooked to a ring at the other end.

Dog-basket.—Used by the steward for the leavings from the cabin table.

Dogger.—A two masted Dutch smack.

Dogsbody.—A mess made of pea-soup, powdered biscuit, and slush.

Dog's ear or **Dog's lug.**—The part of a leech-rope of a top-sail between the head and reef-earing cringles.

Dog-sleep.—Short naps taken when a man should be awake.

Dog-vane.—A small flag or streamer at the mast-head or at the side to indicate the direction of the wind.

Dog-watch.—A subdivision of the usual four hours' watch, so as to bring about a change of watches among the crew. The dog-watches are from 4 to 6, and from 6 to 8 p.m. They are called the first and second dog-watch.

Doldrums.—A belt of calms and light shifting winds close to the equator on either side.

Dollop.—A lump, a piece: as "a dollop of duff."

Dolly.—A tool used in riveting the plates of an iron ship.

Donkey.—A sailor's chest.

Donkey-boiler.—A boiler to work steam-winches, &c.

Donkey-engine.—A supplementary engine for doing work independent of the ship's engines.

Donkey-frigate.—A ship-sloop of twenty-eight guns.

Double.—To round a headland. "Double the Horn," to sail round it.

Double altitudes.—A method of finding the latitude by two observed altitudes.

Double-bottom.—Iron plates inside covering the frames and girders of an iron ship; the space between is called the double-bottom.

Double capstan.—A capstan that can be worked both on an upper and lower deck at once.

Double strop.—A long single strop doubled.

Double top-sails.—Formerly the top-sails were whole sails. They are now divided by being bent to two yards, so that when the halliards of the upper topsail yard are let go, the lower top-sail represents a close-reefed sail.

Double wheel.—Two wheels one abaft the other, fixed on the same spindle, to enable two sets of men to steer the vessel when power is wanted there.

Double whip.—A tackle composed of two double-blocks, the upper one fixed, the lower one movable.

Doughboy.—Pronounced doboy. A small dumpling made of flour and slush.

Dowel.—A piece of brass inserted in the sheave of a block to save it from injury from the pin on which the sheave revolves. Also a piece of hard wood used in scarphing two timbers.

Dowel-bit.—A tool for cutting the holes for the dowels.

Dowelling.—A method of uniting timbers.

Downhauls.—Ropes used for hauling down a jib or stay-sail.

Dowse.—To extinguish, to put out.

Dowse the glim.—Put out the light.

Drabler.—Canvas laced to the bonnet of a sail.

Draft of hands.—Men sent from one ship of war to another, to complete the latter's complement.

Dragging.—A propeller is said to "drag" when the sails urge the vessel faster than the revolutions of the screw can propel her.

Dragging on her.—Said of a man who presses his vessel with canvas in a strong wind.

Draught.—The draught of a ship is the delineation of the various sections of her by line. Also the depth of water she takes to float in.

Drawing the boxes.—Removing the pump-gear in order to drop the sounding-rod to ascertain what water there is in the well.

Dredger.—A boat furnished with a kind of scraper called a dredge for catching oysters, &c. Also a vessel for cleansing harbours and the mouths of rivers.

Dress.—To dress a ship is to decorate her with flags.

Drift.—A tool used in iron ship-building for forcing into rivet-holes which do not lie fair, so that the rivets may enter. Also the rate at which a current runs in the hour. Also to move helplessly with the wind and seas.

Drift-ice.—Detached pieces of ice through which a ship can sail.

Drift-net.—A large net with one-inch meshes, used for catching pilchards, herrings, &c.

Drip-pipe.—In a marine engine, a small pipe connected with the waste steam-pipe, and used for carrying off the condensed steam and hot water which have found their way into the "trap" at the top.

Drive.—To scud at the mercy of a gale.

Driver.—Another name for the spanker or mizzen.

Drogher.—A small West Indian vessel that carries passengers and trades among the ports of those islands.

Drogue.—A large bag made of canvas, thrown overboard to keep a ship head to wind or to deaden her way.

Drop.—The depth of a sail in the centre of it.

Druggs.—Two thick squares of wood clinched together and fitted in a whale-boat, to which is attached a line, one end of which is looped for immediately fastening to a harpoon.

Drum.—A frame of canvas hoisted as a storm warning.

Drumhead.—The top of a capstan.

Drum-hogsheads.—Hogsheads of liquor from which a third of the contents have been stolen.

Druxy.—Plank or timber in a decayed or spongy state.

Dry gale.—A storm of wind under a blue sky.

Dry provisions.—The term applied to tea, flour, sugar, peas, &c.

Dubb.—To smooth down wood with an adze.

Duck.—A kind of fine canvas.

Duck-up!—Haul up the clew of a sail.

Duff.—A pudding made of flour and slush, boiled in a canvas bag.

Dug-out.—A large West African canoe.

Dumb-blocks.—Blocks made of metal, used instead of dead-eyes.

Dumb-chalder.—A piece of metal on the stern-post for the rudder-pintle to rest on.

Dumb craft.—A vessel, such as a barge or lump, without sails.

Dummy.—A piece of strong upright wood on the deck of a smack, to which the trawl-warp is attached when fishing.

Dump.—A bolt for fastening planks.

Dungaree.—A light material worn as dress by sailors.

Dunhead.—A kind of barge.

Dunnage.—Pieces of wood upon which cargo is stowed to keep it clear of the wet at the bottom of the hold.

Dustoree.—Custom paid to a crimp in the East Indies.

Dutch caper.—In olden times a Dutch privateer.

Dutchify.—To dutchify a ship is to alter her square stern into a circular or elliptical one.

Dutchman.—A sailor's name for Scandinavians and Germans as well as Dutchmen.

E

Earing.—There are two kinds of earing. Head-earing is a rope at the upper corner of a sail to secure it to the yard-arm. Reef-earing is a rope on the leech of a sail to secure it to the yard when reefed.

Ears.—The ears of a boat are outside knee-pieces forward.

Earth compass.—A compass placed in a cask filled with earth, to nullify the local attraction on board iron vessels.

Ease.—To pay out or slacken a rope gently.

Ease her!—A command to reduce the motion of an engine.

Ease the helm!—A command to shift the helm by a spoke or two to "meet the sea," as it is called.

Ease up!—To slacken a tackle fall. To "come up" with a rope.

Easter.—The wind easters when it veers to the eastwards.

Easting.—The amount of progress made to the eastwards.

Easy!—Gently! not too fast!

Ebb.—The fall of the tide from the height of the flood.

Eccentric gear.—A method of giving motion to the levers of a marine engine by admitting steam alternately into the steam-ports of the cylinder.

Ecliptic.—A great circle in the heavens which the sun appears to pass over in the course of a year.

Edge down.—To bear down upon an object by keeping the ship gradually and almost imperceptibly away.

Eduction-pipe.—A pipe in a marine steam-engine that conveys steam from the exhaust-side of the cylinder piston into the condenser.

Eight-man boat.—A Faroese whale-boat.

Eiking.—A piece of wood to make up a length.

Elbow.—Two crosses in a ship's cables, when she is moored, caused by her swinging.

Elevator.—A contrivance for loading ships with grain.

Elliot's eye.—A loop in a hemp cable fitted with a thimble and served.

Embargo.—A prohibition on a ship to leave a port.

Embark.—To enter into a ship.

End for end.—When a rope is unrove.

End on.—Said of a ship when only her bows or stern can be seen.

En flute.—A ship is said to be armed en flute when a portion of her guns are taken out and she is used as a transport.

Engine-bearers.—Portions of the seat for supporting the engines and boilers of a steamer. Also called engine-seating.

Engineer.—A person who has charge of the engines and is lord of the engine-room, and very often of the whole ship. There are two grades—first-class and second-class engineers, each of of whom are certificated. Every steamer of over 100-horse power must carry a first and second class engineer: under that power, an only or first engineer, who must be certificated.

Engineer Surveyor.—A person appointed to report upon the efficiency of the machinery of steam-ships.

Enlarge.—Said of the wind when it draws aft.

Equation of time.—The difference between real and apparent time.

Equinoctial points.—Points where the ecliptic and the equator intersect each other.

Escape-valves.—Weighted valves to allow of the escape of steam or water in the way of the movement of the piston.

Euvrou.—A kind of block for extending the legs of a crow-foot. See Crowfoot.

Even keel.—Said when neither end of a ship afloat is lower or higher than the other.

Every stitch.—All the canvas that a vessel carries.

Examinations.—In the merchant service officers are examined in seamanship and navigation, to prove their qualifications for the ranks to which they aspire. The qualifications may be briefly condensed as follows for foreign-going service:—

Second Mate.—He must be seventeen years of age, and have been four years at sea. He must write a legible hand, understand the first five rules of arithmetic, and the use of logarithms; be able to work a day's work, correct the sun's declination for longitude, find his latitude by the sun, with other such problems; and understand all about the rigging and unrigging of ships, stowage, the rule of the road, signals, log-line, &c.

Only Mate.—Must be nineteen years of age, and have been five years at sea. More knowledge is expected in him than in a second mate, for in addition he must be able to calculate the amplitude of the sun, and deduce from it the variation of the compass, find the longitude by chronometer, lay off the place of his ship on the chart, &c., and in seamanship understand all about the ground tackle, keep the ship's log, know the use and management of the rocket apparatus, and so forth.

First Mate.—Must be nineteen years old and have been five years at sea, of which one year must have been either as second or only mate or both. Besides what is required for an only mate, a chief mate must be able to observe azimuths and compute the variation, compare chronometers and keep their rates, work the latitude by single altitude of the sun off the meridian, possess extensive knowledge of seamanship, of the shifting of large spars and sails, of the management of ships in storms, &c.

Master.—Must be twenty-one years old and have been six years at sea, of which at least one year must have been as first or only mate, and one year as second mate. He will be asked more questions than those put to a mate: on magnetic attraction, tides, sounding, jury rudders and rafts, marine law as regards his crew, entry and discharge: also he is expected to know all about charter-parties, Lloyd's agencies, bottomry, and so forth.

Extra Master.—This examination is voluntary. The certificate confers no privilege, and the only use of it is to show that the possessor has a good memory for what he finds in marine guide-books.

Expansion gear.—A contrivance for economizing steam in a marine engine by cutting off steam at any point of the stroke of the piston.

Expansion joints.—Joints fitted in steam pipes so as to allow for expansion and contraction.

Eye.—A loop at the end of a rope, a hole in an iron bolt.

Eye-bolt.—A bolt of iron with an eye in it, sunk into the deck or side as far as the eye.

Eyelet-holes.—Holes in the tablings and reef-bands of a sail for robands, reef-points, cringles, &c.

"Eyes."—This word is applied to holes opening in a sail owing to the force of the wind. "Eyes now showed in the main-topsail, and shortly after it was blown out of the bolt-rope."

Eyes of a vessel.—The foremost point of the forecastle, betwixt the knightheads.

Eye-splice.—An eye formed in a rope by passing its strands through its standing part.

F

Facing.—Setting one piece of timber into another with a rabbet.

Fagged.—This is said of a rope whose end is untwisted.

Fair.—Said of the wind when favourable.

Fair-leader.—A block, thimble, or strip of plank for running gear to lead through.

Fairway.—The navigable part of a river or channel.

Fake.—A single ring of a coil of rope.

Fall.—The hauling part of a tackle.

Fall aboard of.—To drop down foul of another ship.

Fall foul.—To fall foul of a man is to abuse or quarrel with him.

Falling glass.—The sinking of the mercury in a barometer.

Falls.—Tackles for hoisting and lowering boats at the davits.

False-keel.—Pieces of timber below the main keel to protect it in case of taking the ground.

Family boats.—The name given to smacks worked by members of one family.

Fancy-line.—A downhaul rove through a block at the jaws of a gaff.

Fang.—The valve of a pump-box.

Fanning.—Widening the after-part of a ship's top.

Fantod.—A fiddling officer who is always bothering over small things.

Fardage.—Dunnage.

Fast.—To make fast is to attach. "All fast!" a cry to denote that the rope is belayed or a turn taken.

Fast-fish.—A whaling-term, signifying that the whale belongs to the boat's crew that is fast to it.

Fasts.—Wood or stone projections on a quay or pier for mooring vessels to. Also the ropes which hold a vessel.

Favour her!—A call to the helmsman to ease the helm, to let her meet it.

Fay.—To lie close to, as one piece of wood against another.

Fearn.—A small windlass.

Fearnought.—Thick woollen cloth that used to be, and perhaps still is, worn by North-Sea pilots.

Feathering paddle-wheels.—Paddle-wheels of which the boards or floats enter and leave the water in a perpendicular position.

Feathering-screw.—A propeller whose blades can be placed in a direction parallel with the line of the keel. Meant for auxiliaries only.

Feather-white sea.—Said of the sea when covered with foam.

Feed-cock.—A cock near the bottom of a marine boiler for regulating the supply of water to the boiler.

Feeding-engine.—An engine for supplying tubular boilers with feed-water when the large engines are not working.

Feed pipe.—A pipe for introducing water into the boiler to take the place of the water that has passed off in steam.

Feed-pump.—A pump that supplies the boilers of a steamer with water from the hot-well.

Feed-water.—The water with which the boiler is supplied.

Felucca.—A vessel rigged with a lateen sail.

Fend.—To fend off, to save a boat's side from collision or being chafed.

Fenders.—Pieces of timber, or cork, or stuffed canvas over a ship's or boat's side to prevent it from being chafed or injured.

Fetch.—To reach, to arrive at by sailing or steaming: as "we fetched the harbour."

Fetch away.—To break loose, to roll or slide to leeward.

Fetching the pump.—Making it act by pouring water into it.

"Fetch out."—To get out to sea from a bay, harbour, &c., by beating or sailing close.

Fid.—A bar of wood or iron passed through the fid-hole to support a mast.

Fiddle-block.—A double block with one sheave above larger than the lower one.

Fiddle-figurehead, or **Fiddle-head.**—The head of a ship that has no figure, but is decorated with a scroll shaped like a fiddle.

Fiddles.—A framework used to secure the dishes on a cabin table, to prevent them from rolling off.

Fiddley-house.—A barbarous term for the engine-house.

Fid-hole.—A hole in the lower part of all upper mast to receive the fid.

Fife-rail.—A rail round the main-mast fitted with belaying pins. Also the upper fence of the bulwarks of a man-of-war's quarter-deck.

Fighting-lanterns.—See Battle-lanterns.

Fighting-sails.—The canvas on a ship when going into action.

Figure-head.—A bust or figure over a ship's cutwater.

Figure of eight.—A knot shaped like the figure 8 used for preventing a rope from unreeving.

Filler.—A piece of timber to fill up in a made mast.

Fillibuster.—A pirate.

Filling.—In ship-building, wood introduced to make up for a defect in the moulding way.

Filling-room.—Formerly in men-of-war, apartments where powder was filled into cartridges, and furnished with a powder-trough to empty the powder out of the barrels.

Fillings.—Timbers placed between the frames of a ship, fitting close and caulked.

Filling-transom.—A timber above the deck transom for securing the ends of the deck plank, &c.

Fine-weather rolls.—The rolling of a ship under a clear sky in a sea left by a storm.

Finishings.—The name of the quarter-gallery ornamentation.

Finns.—Natives of Finland. These men when members of a ship's company were formerly regarded with great superstition by their shipmates. They were thought to possess the gift of second sight, to hold the winds in control, to keep a bottle of rum full, in spite of hearty pulls at it, a whole voyage.

Fin out.—A whaling expression used when a whale turns over dean.

Fire and lights.—Sailor's nickname for the master-at-arms.

Fire-box.—A space in front of the boilers of a steamer over the furnace doors.

Fireman.—A stoker.

Firemen.—Men stationed at the guns of a man-of-war ready for active duty: their business being to extinguish fire, and also to act as boarders, &c.

Firing-up.—Plying the fires so as to obtain as much steam as possible.

First watch.—The watch from 8 p.m. till midnight.

Fish.—To bind spare booms, planks, &c., to an injured spar to support it. Also to hoist the fluke of an anchor by the fish-tackle, and secure the inner arm and shank by the shank-painter. The anchor is then said to be fished—an operation which follows catting.

Fish-davit.—A piece of timber or iron for hoisting the fluke of an anchor.

Fisherman's bend.—A knot formed by two turns through a ring, a half-hitch and the end stopped.

Fisherman's walk.—"Three steps and overboard," in allusion to the small space offered for walking in smacks, and therefore said of any confined space.

Fish-fag.—A disreputable, foul-mouthed woman.

Fish-hook.—A hook with a pennant for the fish-tackle to be hooked to.

Fish-tackle.—The tackle used in hoisting the fluke of an anchor.

Fit out.—To fit out a ship is to furnish her with masts, sails, anchors, provisions, men, &c.

Five-finger.—The star-fish.

Fixed blocks.—Fixed sheaves in a ship's side.

Flag-officer.—An admiral.

Flag-share.—The admiral's share in captures from an enemy.

Flag-ship.—The ship that carries an admiral's flag.

Flag-staff.—A staff on a vessel's stern.

Flairing.—When the topside of a ship's bows falls outward from the perpendicular.

Flare.—A light made by firing a tar-barrel, &c.

Flare-ups.—Flames shown aboard a vessel as signals.

Flashing-light.—A beacon that shows flashes at short intervals, or groups of flashes at regular intervals.

Flashing-signals.—A method of signalling by means of flashes of light, used in the Royal Navy.

Flash-vessel.—A gaudy-looking but undisciplined ship.

Flat.—A sail is flat when the sheet is hauled down close. Also a sort of lighter, with one mast and a sail like a lug.

Flat-aback.—When the sails are pressed against the mast by the wind.

Flat aft.—Said of the sheets of fore-and-aft sails when hauled as taut as they will go.

Flat-plate keel.—A keel formed of iron plates bent dish-shaped.

Flat-seam.—Two edges of canvas laid over each other and sewn.

Flat-seizing.—A light seizing.

Flatten in.—To tauten the head-sheets.

Flaw.—A sudden burst of wind. Also an opening in a bank of fog.

Fleet.—To come up a tackle for another pull when the blocks have been drawn together. The cry is "Fleet ho!"

Fleeting.—Said of smacks which sail out to the fishing-grounds in fleets.

Flemish coil.—To coil up a rope with the end in the centre and the fakes outside of one another, the whole lying flat.

Flemish eye.—An eye formed in a rope by unlaying one strand and placing the remaining ends against the standing part.

Flemish horses.—Foot-ropes at the yard-arms of topsail and lower yards.

Flench-gut.—Whale blubber in long slices.

Flipper.—The hand.

Float.—A large flat-bottomed boat.

Floating coffin.—A rotten vessel.

Floating dock.—A fabric that is made to sink in order to receive a ship, and then to float so as to raise its burden above water. Also a wet dock.

Floating light.—A light-ship.

Floating on cargo.—Said of a vessel full of water, but kept afloat by her cargo, such as timber, cork, oil, &c.

Floating stage.—A platform on the water for painters, caulkers, &c.

Floats.—The boards or paddles fitted to the wheels of paddle steamers.

Flogging the glass.—Said of the old glasses used to denote time, when shaken to make the sand run.

Flood.—High water.

Floor-guide.—A timber between the floor and the keel.

Floor-plans.—Longitudinal sections of the water-lines and ribband-lines.

Floor-plates.—Formerly plates in the bottom of an iron ship corresponding with the floor-timbers in wooden ones.

Floor-ribband.—A timber for the support of the floors of a ship.

Flotsam.—Goods lost by shipwreck and floating on the sea.

Flow.—To let go the sheet of a head-sail.

Flowing sheet.—The sheet well eased off when the wind is abaft the beam.

Flue boiler.—A marine boiler constructed to confine the flame and hot gases generated in the furnace in narrow flues.

Flues.—Passages in a steamer's boiler for heated air.

Fluke.—The end of each arm of an anchor.

Flunkey.—Sailor's name for the ship's steward.

Flurry.—The death-throes of a whale.

Flush.—Level, clear of incumbrance. Also, level with.

Flush-decked.—Having a clear sweep of deck.

Flush-scuttles.—Apertures whose framework is nearly level with the deck.

Flush-up.—Said of cargo that comes up to a level with the hatches.

Fly.—The length of a flag from the point of suspension and the extremity. Also the compass card before it is mounted.

Fly-away.—A mirage or fictitious appearance of land.

Fly-block.—A topsail tie-block.

Fly-boat.—A flat-bottomed Dutch vessel.

Fly-by-night.—A square sail formerly used by sloops when running.

Flying bridge.—An elevated bridge on steamers, forward of the funnel.

Flying-jib.—A fore-and-aft sail that sets on a stay from the foretopgallant masthead to the flying-jib boom end.

Flying-jib boom.—A continuation of the jib boom for the flying-jib to set on.

Flying kites.—The lofty sails used in light weather, such as sky-sails, royal and topgallant studding-sails, &c.

Flying moor.—Letting go a weather anchor whilst the ship has way, and then, when the cable range is nearly out, letting go the other anchor.

Flying proa.—A vessel belonging to the Ladrone Islands. She is fitted with a large triangular sail attached to two booms which meet at the vessel's head, and she is furnished with a long outrigger.

Flying sky-sail.—A sky-sail that is stowed with the royal. The yard has neither lifts nor braces, and the clews are secured to the royal yard-arms.

Flying-to.—Coming up into the wind swiftly.

Fly-wheel pumps.—Pumps fitted with wheels, of which the revolutions greatly facilitate the labour of pumping.

Fog-dog.—A break in a fog. See Flaw.

Foggy.—Slightly drunk. Muddled with drink.

Fog-horn.—An instrument that delivers a powerful note as a signal in fogs. Worked by the mouth, bellows, and by steam.

Fo'ksle hand.—The same as fore-mast hand.

Foot.—The bottom of a sail.

Footing.—A fee exacted by sailors from one who goes aloft for the first time.

Foot-rails.—Mouldings on a ship's stern.

Foot-rope.—A rope suspended under a yard or boom for men to stand on. Also the rope at the bottom of a sail.

Foot-sugar.—A mixture of dirt and molasses served out to merchant sailors.

Foot-valve.—In a marine engine, a flat piece of metal in the passage between the condenser and air-pump.

Foot-waling.—Inside planking over the floor timbers.

Fore.—The forward part of a ship, or what is forward, as fore-mast, fore-hatch, fore-sail, &c. At the fore, means at the fore-royal mast-head.

Fore and after.—A cocked hat. Also a fore-and-aft rigged vessel.

Fore-and-aft schooner.—A schooner without square yards.

Fore-bowline.—A rope to haul out the weather leech of the fore-course.

Fore-braces.—The ropes by which the fore-yard of a ship, barque, or brig is swung.

Forecastle.—A compartment where sailors live, in the bows of a ship. Also the deck over the compartment is called the forecastle. In old marine works this is defined as a place fitted for a close fight on the upper deck forward.

Fore-course.—The fore-sail of a ship.

Forefoot.—The foremost part of the keel.

Fore-ganger.—A piece of rope attached to a harpoon.

Fore-guy.—A rope to steady the lower studding-sail swinging boom.

Fore-hold.—The hold between the main-hold and fore-peak.

Foreign-going.—Ships bound to ports outside the home-trade limits.

Fore-lock.—A piece of iron driven into the end of a bolt.

Fore-mast.—The lower mast nearest the bows of a ship.

Fore-mast hand.—A man serving before the mast.

Forenoon watch.—The watch from 8 a.m. till noon.

Fore-peak.—The hold in the bows.

Fore-rake.—The rake of the stem.

Fore-reach.—To shoot ahead in stays. To pass when close-hauled another vessel close-hauled.

Fore-royal.—The sail above the topgallant sail.

Fore-royal mast.—The mast above the fore-topgallant mast.

Fore-runner.—A small piece of red bunting or cloth on a log-line marking the inboard end of the stray. See Stray line.

Fore-sail.—The lowest square sail on the fore-mast of a ship, barque, or brig. In a schooner it is a gaff fore-and-aft sail. In a cutter it is a jib-shaped sail.

Fore-scuttle.—A hatch by which the forecastle is entered.

Fore-sheet.—The ropes by which the lee corner of the fore-sail is hauled aft.

Fore-sheet horse.—An iron bar for the sheet of a sloop's fore-sail to travel on.

Fore-skysail.—A small square sail above the fore-royal.

Fore-skysail mast.—The mast or pole above the fore-royal mast.

Fore-tack.—The ropes which keep the weather corner of the fore-sail down.

Fore-topgallant mast.—The mast above the fore-topmast.

Fore-topgallant sail.—The sail above the fore-topsail.

Fore-topgallant studding-sail.—A sail set at the fore-topgallant yard-arm, and extended by a boom on the fore-topsail yard.

Fore-topgallant studding-sail boom.—A boom on the fore-topsail yard which extends the foot of the studding-sail of that name.

Fore-topmast.—The mast above the fore-mast.

Fore-topmast stay-sail.—A fore-and-aft sail that sets on a stay from the fore-topmast head to the bowsprit.

Fore-topmast studding-sail.—A sail set at the fore-topsail yard-arm, and the foot extended by a boom on the lower yard.

Fore-topmast studding-sail boom.—A boom on the fore-yard for extending the foot of the studding-sail so called.

Fore-topmen.—Hands stationed in the fore-top of a man-of-war, to attend to the sails and rigging above it.

Fore-topsail.—The sail that sets above the fore-sail in square-rigs.

Fore-yard.—The lowest yard on the fore-mast.

Forge.—To shoot ahead.

Forkers.—Dockyard thieves.

Forrard.—Forward.

Forward there!—The exclamation when the forecastle is hailed.

Fother.—To stop a leak by drawing a sail filled with oakum, rubbish, &c., under a vessel.

Foul.—Anything twisted, anything that will not run is called foul. To foul a vessel is to collide with her and get locked. In olden times foul was used for storm: as "foul stay-sail," for "storm stay-sail."

Foul anchor.—When the cable is twisted round the anchor.

Foul hawse.—When the two cables get crossed.

Founder.—A vessel founders when she sinks.

Four-cant.—A four-stranded rope.

Foxes.—Rope-yarns twisted and rubbed with tarred canvas.

Fox-key.—A key with a wedge of metal fitted into the end to secure it in its place.

Frame.—The portion of a ship that consists of her form or shape.

Frap.—To bind by passing ropes round.

Free.—Sailing with the yards braced in.

Freeboard.—The side a vessel shows out of water.

Free-trader.—A class of vessels built to seek employment wherever there was most to be earned. They came into existence after the East Indian trade had been thrown open.

Fresh breeze.—A strong wind.

Freshen.—To ease out chain; to shift a rope so as to relieve it; to alter the position of ballast. Also the wind freshens when it increases.

Freshen hawse.—Paying out a short length of cable to save the chafe. This was a custom when rope cables were used with service on them in the hawse-pipes.

Fresh grub or provisions.—Unsalted meat, baker's bread, &c.

Fresh hand at the bellows.—Said as the wind freshens into a gale.

Fresh water.—Water shipped for drinking, but not always drinkable.

Fresh-water sailor.—A yachtsman. A green hand.

Friction rollers.—Rollers fitted in a block that the sheave may revolve easily.

Friction tube.—A means of firing a gun by ignition through friction of the priming in the tube.

Frigate.—A ship with one whole battery deck.

Frigate-built.—A ship with a waist led to by steps from the quarter-deck and forecastle.

Frigatoon.—A ship-sloop of war.

Fruit-clippers.—Small, fast, handsome schooners which formerly traded between this country and the Mediterranean, in raisins, figs, currants, &c. *Circa* 1845.

Full and bye.—Sailing close to the wind, but keeping every sail full.

Full-bottomed.—A vessel with a wide hold.

Full feather.—Same as full fig.

Full fig.—Full dress. Same as full puff, full feather.

Full for stays!—Keep her full for going about, that she may round handsomely.

Full man.—A coasting term for able seaman.

Full-powered steamer.—A steamer whose engines are powerful enough to do all the work of driving her in all weathers, as distinguished from an auxiliary, whose steam-power is insufficient in strong adverse winds.

Funnel.—The large upright pipe or cylinder on a steamer through which the furnace smoke is expelled.

Funnel-casing.—A portion of the funnel of a steamer extending from the smoke-box to some distance upwards.

Funnel hood.—A projected portion of or protection to the funnel, raised some feet above the deck.

Funnel stays.—Wire or other stays to support the funnel.

Funny.—A clinker-built narrow boat for sculling.

Fur.—Deposit in neglected marine boilers.

Furnace.—Places inside the shell of a boiler for containing the fire.

Fusible plugs.—Plugs which melt at a certain temperature, and thus enable the steam to escape should the safety-valve fail.

Futtock plates.—Iron plates with dead eyes to which the topmast rigging is set up and the futtock shrouds hooked.

Futtocks.—Pieces of timber connected with the floor in the bottom of a ship.

Futtock shrouds.—Iron shrouds leading through the sides of a top and connecting the topmast rigging with the lower mast.

Futtock staff.—A piece of wood or iron crossing the upper part of the shrouds, to secure the catharpen legs to.

G

Gab.—A notch for the pin of the gab-lever on the eccentric rod of a marine steam-engine.

Gabarre.—A French store-ship.

Gabert.—A Scotch barge or lump.

Gad-yang.—A Chinese coaster.

Gaff.—An instrument like a boat-hook used in the blubber-room of whalers. Also a spar for setting a fore-and-aft sail on.

Gaff-topsail.—A fore-and-aft sail set over the lower sails of a schooner, the spanker of a barque, &c.

Gaff-topsail downhaul.—A rope attached to the after-clew of the sail for taking it in.

Gaff-topsail outhaul.—A rope hitched to the clew of the sail and rove through a sheave at the gaff end for hauling the sail out.

Gage.—The position of a vessel as to another, weather-*gage*, lee-*gage*, being to windward of her or to leeward.

Gain.—To gain the wind is to weather a vessel.

Galleas.—A vessel of the sixteenth century, described as long, low, and sharp-built, propelled by oars and sails, and used as a fighting-ship.

Galleries.—Platforms over the stern of ships, with access from the stem windows. Long since disused.

Galley.—A ship's kitchen, formerly called caboose in merchantmen. Also a six or eight oared boat. Also a man-of-wars boat used by the captain.

Galley-built.—A vessel was so called when her waist was only one or two steps in descent from the quarter-deck and forecastle. See Frigate-built.

Galley-growlers.—Loafing, mutinous grumblers.

Galley-punt.—An open sailing-boat used by pilots in the Channel off the Forelands.

Gallied.—Frightened. A whaling term.

Galliot.—A Dutch vessel with round sides, two-masted, the foremast square-rigged.

Gallows-bitts.—Cross pieces of timber on which spare booms and spars are stowed.

Game-ship.—Formerly a ship whose captain and mates could be corrupted by bribes to allow the cargo to be stolen.

Gamming.—A whaleman's term for the visits paid by crews to one another at sea.

Gammoning.—Lashings to secure the bowsprit to the cutwater.

Gammon-knee.—A knee-timber bolted to the stem under the bowsprit.

Gang.—A number of a crew told off for a particular job.

Gangboard.—A platform on a man-of-war that connected the quarter-deck with the forecastle.

Gang-cask.—A 32-gallon cask. A cask for bringing water on board in boats.

Ganger.—Lengths of chain cable shackled to the sheet anchor.

Gangway.—A part of the vessel's side, nearly amidships, by which people enter and leave a ship.

Gangway ladder.—A ladder over the side by which a ship is entered.

Gantline.—A girtline.

Garlands.—Fastenings formed of small stuff, used in taking in and out a mast.

Garnet.—A purchase for hoisting cargo.

Garters.—The irons in which a man's legs are confined.

Gaskets.—Pieces of rope or sennit affixed to a yard, to pass round a sail to secure it when rolled up.

Gas-pipes.—The name given to those long, narrow iron steamers, whose length is nine or ten times the breadth of the beam. Formerly the length of ships rarely exceeded four-and-a-half or five times the beam.

Gather.—To haul in; as, gather in the slack, gather aft that sheet.

Gather way.—Said of a ship when she begins to move.

Gauntlet.—A rope to which hammocks are attached to dry after being scrubbed.

General average.—When a portion of a cargo is sacrificed, the remainder that is saved becomes subject to general average.

Geordie.—Nickname for a north-country collier.

Ghaut serang.—A shipping agent or crimp in the East Indies.

Gib.—A fixed iron wedge for tightening the straps and brasses of the different bearings in a marine engine.

Gift-rope.—A fast for a boat at the guess-warp boom.

Gig.—A small boat that used to hang by stern-davits, and called the captain's gig, because used in harbour by the master of the ship.

Gilguy.—A term applied by seamen to anything they forget the name of.

Gimbal.—A ring that keeps the compass horizontal by moving freely on an axis within which it swings at right angles.

Gimblet.—To turn an anchor on its stock.

Gin.—An iron block, the sheave working in a cross.

Ginger-bread quarters.—Living in luxury—at least from a sailor's point of view.

Girtline.—A whip purchase used for hoisting up rigging.

Give way!—An order to men who are rowing to pull with more force.

Gland.—A collar in a marine engine for encircling the piston and air-pump rod, &c., used for holding oil for lubricating and for compressing the packing of the stuffing-box it is screwed to.

Glass.—A telescope. Also the sand-glass used in heaving the reel-log.

Glass water-gauge.—A glass tube attached to the marine boiler by brass fittings, and furnished with cocks to show the height of the water in the boiler.

Glim.—A light.

Glip.—The oily wake a sperm-whale, when alarmed, leaves behind it.

Glut.—A piece of canvas with an eyelet-hole sewed in a sail near the head.

Go below.—To leave the deck. A term for dismissing the watch below after all hands have been on deck.

Go below the watch.—An order intimating that the division of the crew whose turn it is to be below are no longer wanted on deck.

Gob-line.—A rope leading from the martingale.

Going about.—The act of tacking.

Going free.—Sailing with the wind on or abaft the beam.

Going large.—Sailing with the wind on the quarter.

Gone.—Loosened. "All gone!" means the rope is let go.

Good crop.—Formerly said of a deck that was much arched.

Goose-neck.—An iron outrigger to support a boom.

Goose-wing.—A fore-and-aft vessel running with the gaff fore-sail guyed out on one side and the main-sail on the other.

Goose-winged.—When the weather clew of a course is down and the lee clew and buntlines hauled up.

Gores.—The angles of the cloths which widen or deepen a sail.

Goring-cloths.—Pieces of canvas to widen a sail.

Grab.—An Indian coaster.

Grade.—A degree of rank.

Grafting.—The ornamentation of a rope's end by making nettles of the strands.

Grain.—To be *in the grain of another skip* was an old-fashioned way of explaining that you were sailing ahead of her lying the same course.

Grain cargoes.—Any kind of grain: corn, rice, paddy, pulse, seeds, nuts, or nut kernels.

Granny's bend.—A hitch that slips.

Grape.—Cast-iron shot packed in canisters.

Grappling-irons.—Irons used in fighting to hold ships together.

Grasp.—The handle of an oar.

Grass-comber.—A countryman shipped as a sailor.

Gratings.—A species of thick wooden lattice to cover hatches, or for decoration.

Grave.—To clean.

Graving-dock.—A dock which admits of a vessel being placed in it and grounded.

Great circle sailing.—The sailing by which the direct course to a place is to be shaped.

Greave.—To clean a ship's bottom by burning.

Green sea.—A mass of water rolling over a ship without breaking.

Grenade.—An explosive ignited by a fusee and thrown by the hand.

Gripe.—A portion of a wooden ship's forefoot. To *gripe* is for a ship to show a tendency to come up into the wind.

Gripes.—Supports for securing a quarter-boat as she hangs at the davits.

Grog.—Understood by sailors to mean rum drunk neat or with water.

Grog-blossom.—A nose reddened by drink. Also a pimple due to drink.

Groggy.—Half drunk.

Grommet.—A ring of rope.

Gross tonnage.—The aggregate cubic space in a ship below her uppermost deck, and in permanent closed-in spaces on her uppermost deck, which are used for cargo, stores, accommodation of passengers and crew, &c.

Ground-rope.—A rope on the under part of a trawl that drags along the bottom.

Ground-tackle.—A term that includes the anchoring apparatus.

Ground-tier.—The lowest range of casks in the hold.

Ground-way.—The lower piece of the tiers of blocks on which the keel of a ship is laid.

Grow.—A cable grows according as the ship stretches it from the anchor on one or the other bow.

Growl.—To complain, to grumble.

Guarantee engineer.—The name given to an engineer who is appointed by the engine builder, but paid by the owner of the steamer. The system is most injurious to discipline, as a "guarantee engineer" seldom considers himself under any obligation to obey or even to take notice of the captain's orders.

Gudgeons.—Braces or eyes fixed to the stern-post, to receive the pintles of a rudder.

Guess-warp.—A rope to secure a boat to a swinging boom.

Guffy.—A soldier.

Guineaman.—A slaver.

Gulletting of rudder.—Spaces allowed between the pintles and the rudder where there are scores or indents to permit of the shipping and unshipping of the rudder.

Gun-fire.—The morning or evening guns.

Gun-gear.—Left-handed rope used for securing cannons on board ship.

Gunner.—A warrant officer who has charge of the ammunition, &c., in a ship of war. In the seventeenth century the post of gunner was very highly valued. He wore his sword on shore, kept company with the commissioned officers, was in receipt of whole pay, though he never went out of harbour, and if in action the commanding officers of a ship fell, the gunner took command.

Gunner's daughter.—The gun to which boys were lashed for punishment.

Gunner's mate.—A gunner's assistant.

Gun-room.—The compartment in a ship of war occupied by the junior officers.

Guns.—An old expression signifying violent blasts of wind. "The guns were at times so violent that the sea appeared like precipices under their stern." Hence the expression "Blowing great guns."

Gun-tackle purchase.—A tackle consisting of two single blocks, each fitted with a hook.

Gunwale.—The place where a ship's upper deck touches the sides. Also the upper rail of a boat or vessel. Chiefly applied to boats.

Gurnet.—A pendant and tackle used for hoisting guns.

Gurnet-pendant.—A rope used in hoisting the breech of a gun.

Gurry.—A dark glutinous substance found on the back of the Greenland or right whale.

Gutted.—A gutted ship is a vessel whose inside is cleaned out of all fittings, &c., by the sea or by fire.

Guys.—Ropes acting as side supports of a boom.

Gyb.—The old spelling of the word "jib." Hence, no doubt. The term gybing or jibing, formerly spelt and pronounced *jibbing*.

Gyver.—An old name for a double block.

H

Hail.—To call to another, to "sing out."

Half-breadth plan.—A drawing descriptive of half of the longest and widest level section in a ship.

Half-crown.—The ends of a rope crossed, and seized at the crossing to form an eye.

Half-gunshot.—Said of a ship passing within half the distance that can be covered by the shot of her enemy.

Half-hitch.—The end of a rope taken round the standing part and passed through the bight.

Half-laughs and purser's grins.—Sneers. Half-and-half meanings.

Half-marrows.—Inferior seamen.

Half-mast.—The situation of a flag lowered in respect.

Half-pike.—A small pike formerly used in boarding a ship.

Half-ports.—Shutters for the upper part of a gun-port.

Half seas over.—Half drunk.

Half-topsail.—A sail that sets with a gaff above the square-sail of a cutter.

Halliards.—Ropes to hoist yards, sails, flags, &c.

Hammock.—A piece of canvas fitted with a number of small ropes at each end, and slung up so as to form a bed.

Hammock-berthing.—The disposition in a man-of-war of the hammocks when stowed, as, for instance, the forecastle men forward, fore-topmen, main-topmen, &c., aft, quartermasters in the tiers.

Hammock-cloth.—Protection for the hammocks against wet when stowed in the nettings.

Hammock-nettings.—Stout nettings on deck in which the hammocks are stowed, and which in an action form a defence against musketry, &c.

Hand.—To furl, to stow sails. Also a sailor, one of a crew.

Hand-grommets.—Loops of rope worked round the jackstay of royal and topgallant yards for men to hold on by.

Handing-rooms.—Rooms in a man-of-war through which gun-powder is conveyed in fearnought shoots, that it may not pass straight on deck from the magazine.

Handle.—To handle a ship is to sail and manoeuvre her.

Hand-lead.—A lead of from 7 lbs. to 14 lbs. in weight.

Hand-line.—A lead-line.

Hand-masts.—Pieces of wood used in the construction of large sheers.

Hand over hand.—Dragging on a rope quickly with alternate hands.

Hand-pump.—A pump for getting water, beer, &c., out of casks.

Handsomely!—A cry to signify smartly, *but* carefully.

Handsomely over the bricks!—An exclamation signifying "go cautiously, mind how you walk."

Hand-spike.—A lever of wood used in heaving round a windlass.

Handy Billy.—A name for the watch-tackle.

Handy ship.—A ship that is easy to work, that steers well, whose running-gear travels easily, &c.

Hanging-blocks.—Blocks through which the topsail-ties reeve.

Hanks.—Rings by which a fore-and-aft sail slides up and down the stay.

Harbour-bunt.—The bunt of a sail neatly stowed and well triced up.

Harbour-dues.—The charges for using a harbour.

Harbour-gaskets.—Short gaskets for giving a furled sail a handsome look.

Harbour-master.—An official who is responsible for the management of a harbour, the berthing of vessels in it, &c.

Harbour-work.—Remarks entered in a log when the ship is in port.

Hard a lee.—When the rudder is brought over to windward as far as it will go.

Hard a port.—When the rudder is brought over to starboard as far as it will go.

Hard a starboard.—The contrary of hard a port.

Hard a weather.—The contrary of hard a lee.

Hard case.—A severe, brutal mate or officer.

Hard gale.—A fierce gale.

Hard up.—When the rudder is brought over to leeward as far as it will go.

Harmattan.—A periodical wind encountered in the Gulf of Guinea, blowing from the north-east.

Harness cask.—A kind of cask on deck, in which the salt meat is kept for the immediate use of the men.

Harpins.—In wooden ships harpins are the ribbands formed of oak or elm plank at the extremities of the vessel. In iron ships they are made of angle-irons furnished with holes for securing the frames.

Harpoon.—A barbed iron instrument used in whaling, &c. A *live harpoon* is a harpoon in use.

Hatch.—An opening in the deck for admission into the interior of the ship.

Hatch-boat.—A small vessel whose deck consists almost wholly of hatches.

Hat-money.—Payment to a shipmaster for the care of goods.

Haul.—To pull.

Haul-bowline.—A seaman.

Haul out.—To warp out: as haul out of dock.

Haul out to leeward!—A cry in reefing, to denote that the weather-earing is passed.

Haul the wind.—To turn a ship so as to bring the wind forward.

Hawk's bill.—A small turtle with a mouth like a hawk's bill.

Hawse-bags.—Bags for plugging the hawse-pipes.

Hawse-holes.—Holes in the bows through which the cables pass.

Hawse-pipe.—Iron piping in the hawse-holes to save the wood from chafing.

"Hawse-pipe sailor."—A man before the mast. One who starts in the profession from the forecastle.

Hawse-plugs.—Plugs for the hawse-pipes when the cables are unshackled and stowed away, to prevent the water from washing through them.

Hawse-timbers.—The timbers next the knightheads for the reception of the hawse-holes.

Hawser.—A large rope used for towing, &c.

Hawser-laid.—When the strands are laid from left to right.

Haze.—To punish with extra or unnecessary work.

Head.—The upper end of a spar. The bows of a ship. The top of a sail.

Head-clew.—The part of a hammock where the occupant's head rests.

Head-earing.—A rope for bending the upper corner of a square sail to the yard.

Head-earing strop.—A strop at a yard-arm for bending the sail to.

Head-ledges.—Transverse hatch-coamings.

Head-pump.—A pump in the bows, used for washing down the decks.

Head-sails.—The jibs, fore-topmast stay-sail, &c.

Head-sea.—Waves running against a ship's course.

Head to wind.—Lying with the bows facing the wind.

Headway.—A vessel's direct passage through the water.

Head-wind.—Wind that prevents a ship heading her course. Wind directly in the path of a vessel.

Hearty.—My hearty, a stage term applied to a sailor.

Heart-yarns.—The centre yarns of a strand.

Heave and paul!—An exclamation to encourage the men at a capstan or windlass.

Heave and raise the dead!—Said in heaving up the anchor.

Heaver.—A short wooden bar used as a purchase.

Heave the lead.—An order to sound with the hand-lead.

Heave the log.—An order to measure the vessel's speed with the log-line and glass.

Heaving down.—Heeling a ship by dragging her down with tackles affixed to the mast-heads.

Heavy metal.—Large guns.

Heck-boat.—A one-masted clinker-built boat.

Heel.—The lower end of a spar. *To heel* is to lie over, as in a breeze.

Heel-brace.—An iron support at the bottom of a rudder.

Heel-chain.—A chain from the bowsprit cap round the heel of the jib boom.

Heeling.—The lower end of a mast where the fid-hole is.

Heeling error.—An error in the compass of an iron ship due to her heeling to starboard or port. With her head to the *northward* on the starboard tack easterly deviation is increased, on the port tack westerly deviation is increased. Heading *south*, westerly deviation is increased on the starboard tack, and easterly deviation on the port tack.

Heel-lashing.—A rope to secure the inboard end of a boom.

Heel-rope.—A rope for securing the inner end of a studding-sail boom to the yard.

Heels.—She has good heels, said of a swift ship.

Hell afloat.—A ship officered by brutal men.

Helm.—A term for all the steering arrangements of a ship.

Helm-port.—The aperture in the counter in which the rudder-head works.

Helm-port transom.—A timber to strengthen the helm-port.

Helm's a lee!—The cry in tacking to intimate that the helm is down, and that the head-sails are to be flowed.

Hen-frigate.—A ship was so called when the captain's wife influenced the routine, &c.

Hermaphrodite brig.—A two-masted vessel, brig-rigged forward, and fore-and-aft rigged aft.

Hide-rope.—Made from hide.

High and dry.—Out of water.

High latitudes.—Parallels towards the poles.

High pressure.—A method of disposing of used-up steam by letting it out by an escape valve.

Hitch.—To knot, to fasten. A hitch is a manner of making a rope fast. There are many different kinds, such as a *timber-hitch*, a *rolling hitch*, a *Blackwall hitch*, a *marlin-spike hitch*, &c. Also to hitch up the breeches, to pull them up.

Hitcher.—A boat-hook.

Ho—A sailor's cry for stop.

Hobbler.—A long-shore man of all work.

Hog.—A kind of scrubbing-brush.

Hog-back.—A frame of timbers joined together in the shape of a bow to compensate by strength for the want of depth of side.

Hogged.—A vessel is *hogged* when the middle part of her bottom is so strained as to curve upwards.

Hold.—The internal lower part of the hull of a ship.

Holding on to the slack.—Idling.

Holding water.—Checking a boat's way by keeping the blades of the oars stationary in the water.

Holding on with his eyelids.—Said of a man aloft-with nothing much to lay hold of.

Holidays.—Places left untarred on shrouds, backstays, &c., during the operation of tarring them.

Hollow sea.—Yawning waters after a gale.

Holophone.—A device for concentrating and directing the waves of sound for fog-signals.

Holy-stone—A stone used for cleaning a ship's decks.

Home.—To sheet home, to drag the corners of the sails to the yard-arms. To come home, said of the anchor when, on the windlass being manned, it comes to the ship instead of the ship going to it.

Home-trade passenger-ship.—Any ship carrying passengers trading to English port, and within the limits included between the River Elbe and Brest.

Homeward-bounder.—A ship sailing to the country she belongs to.

Housing.—All that part of the mast that extends from the heel to where it becomes visible on deck.

Housing a mast.—To snug a mast by lowering it without removing the rigging.

Hood.—A covering for a hatch, a binnacle, &c.

Hood-ends.—Ends of the planks which fit into the stem and stern posts.

Hook and butt.—The ends of timbers overlaying one another.

Hook-bolts.—Fitted to fasten lower deck ports.

Hooker.—A little smack that fishes with lines and hooks. Also a term applied by sailors to their vessels.

Hook-pot.—A kind of can with a hook for hanging to the edge of a bunk, &c., in which sailors bring their tea from the galley.

Hoppers.—A species of barge, usually built of iron and sometimes propelled by steam, used for carrying the mud dredged out of harbours, &c., to sea.

Horizon.—The sea-line that bounds the view of the spectator on the ocean.

Horns.—Outer ends of the cross-trees.

Horse.—A foot-rope. A breast-rope for a leadsman. An iron bar for a sheet to slide upon. A jack-stay.

Horse-latitudes.—A space north of the trade-winds in the Atlantic, where the winds are baffling.

Horse-marine.—A lubber.

Horse-power.—33,000 lbs., an expression indicative of the capacity of a steam-engine.

Horses.—The old term for foot-ropes.

Horse-shoe.—A piece of rope spliced into each leg of a pair of shrouds.

Hose.—A length of tubing for washing down the decks and for other purposes.

Hot-coppers.—The parched throat after a night's debauch.

Hot-press.—The impressing of seamen without regard to their protections.

Hot-well.—A tank in a marine engine to receive the water pumped from the condenser by the air-pump.

Hounding.—All that part of the mast that extends from the deck to where the rigging is placed.

Hounds.—The upper part of the cheeks of a mast.

House-flag.—A flag denoting the firm to which the ship belongs.

Hoveller.—A man who furnishes chains, anchors, &c., to vessels which have lost theirs.

Hove short!—The cry to denote that the cable is up and down.

Hove-to.—The situation of a ship when her way is arrested by backing some of the sails and leaving the others full. A ship is sometimes hove-to in a storm under bare poles, that is, by bracing one set of yards forward and the others aft. Steamers are commonly hove-to head to sea, their engines slowly revolving. There is now a fashion coming in of heaving long steamers to *stern on* to the sea.

Huddock.—A cabin.

Hug.—To keep close to the wind in sailing.

Hulk.—A condemned hull, though it may be used.

Hull.—The fabric of a ship without her masts.

Hull-down.—Said of a ship when her hull is hidden behind the sea.

Hulled.—A vessel is said to be hulled when a ball strikes or lodges in her side.

Hunk.—To live with, to share with.

Hurrah's nest.—"A hurrah's nest—everything at top and nothing at bottom," signifying the utmost confusion, that nothing wanted is to be found.

Hurricane-house.—A square of canvas in the weather rigging, to protect the officer of the watch when the ship is hove-to in a bitter gale.

Hutch-hooks.—Small cleats used in ship-building.

Hygrometer.—An instrument for showing the degree of moisture or dampness in the air.

I

Ice-bound.—The situation of a vessel prevented from proceeding on her voyage by being surrounded with ice.

Ice-floe.—Masses of ice, such as pack, stream, or drift ice, broken from the solid surface by the swell of the ocean and sent adrift.

"I didn't come through the cabin windows."—Meaning that the speaker learnt his profession in the forecastle.

"I'd weather him out, if he was the devil himself."—Meaning that the speaker will stick to the ship and draw his wages, let the captain treat him as ill as he chooses.

Immersion.—The eclipse or disappearance of a satellite in the shadow of the planet.

Imp.—A length of twisted hair in a fishing-line.

Impress—To force into the naval service of the State.

In.—"In" means "take in," as "in main royal," "in flying-jib."

In-and-out bolts.—Bolts driven into the hanging and lodging knees through the sides.

In-and-out haulers.—The ropes by which a standing gaff-sail is set or taken in.

Index-error.—Deviation from the coincidence of the reflected and direct images of a heavenly body viewed through a sextant.

Indiaman.—Formerly an East India Company's ship; now any large vessel that trades to the East Indies.

Indicator.—An instrument for measuring the pressure of steam in the cylinder.

Indicator-card.—A card divided into parts, upon which a pencil fixed at the top of the piston-rod marks a diagram showing the relation of the power developed to the consumption of fuel.

In draught.—A current running inwards or shorewards from the sea.

In irons.—A ship is in irons when she is so caught by the wind that in working she will not cast one way or the other.

Injection pipe.—In a marine engine a pipe attached to the condenser for conducting injection water for condensing steam in the cylinder.

Inner and outer turns.—Method of passing the earings in reefing.

Inner jib.—A fore-and-aft sail setting on a stay from the fore-top-mast head to the jib boom.

In-rigger.—A boat that has her rowlocks on the gunwale.

In shore.—Close to the land.

Inter-costal kelsons.—Strong additional fore and aft supports placed outside the angle-irons or ribs of a ship.

Internal safety-valve.—A boiler valve for the introduction of air when the inside pressure grows feeble.

International code.—A code of signals representing a uniform system of signalling at sea, and adopted by England, France, America, Denmark, Holland, Sweden and Norway, Russia, Greece, Italy, Austria, Germany, Spain, Portugal, Brazil, and Belgium.

Invoice.—A document describing goods shipped, together with charges, &c.

Inward charges.—The expenses incurred in entering a port.

Inward desertion.—Desertion of seamen from ships newly arrived in British ports.

Irishman's hurricane.—"An Irishman's hurricane—right up and down," a dead calm.

Irishman's reef.—The head of a sail tied up.

Irish pennants.—Fag-ends of rope, rope-yarns, &c., flying about.

Irish splice.—Turns hove in the lay of a ratlin until shortened in to the required length.

Iron horse.—An iron rod covered with painted canvas affixed to the head boards of a ship.

Issue-room.—A room in a man-of-war where provisions for immediate use are issued.

"It's a good dog nowadays that'll come when he's called; let alone coming before it."—A sailor's excuse for not showing himself until summoned.

"I've been through the mill, ground and bolted."—Signifying that the speaker has had plenty of experience.

Ivory's rule.—A method of solving the problem, "Latitude by double altitudes" of the same body, but applicable only to such bodies as do not change their declination in the interval.

J

Jabble.—"A jabble of a sea," a confused, nasty sea.

Jack.—A flag composed of the union, i.e. St. George's and St. Andrew's cross. Also the name by which sailors are spoken of generally.

Jack Adams.—A fool.

Jackass-barque.—A vessel ship-rigged on the fore-mast, and fore-and-aft rigged on the main-mast.

Jack-block.—A block used in sending topgallant masts up and down.

Jack-boots.—Fishermen's sea-boots.

Jack crosstrees.—Iron crosstrees to support royal masts—out of date.

Jacket-cocks.—Cocks attached to cylinder jackets to free them from condensed water.

Jackets.—Coverings of cylinders of steam-engines.

Jacketting.—A rope's-ending.

Jack in the dust.—Sailor's name for the steward's mate.

Jack-knife.—A knife slung by a laniard and worn by sailors. A knife that closes, in contradistinction to a sheath-knife.

Jack-screw.—An appliance for stowing cotton, bales of wool, &c.

Jackson.—To stop tackles from travelling by jamming the blocks.

Jack-staff.—A staff for a flag on the bowsprit.

Jack-stay.—A bar of iron along the top of a yard to bend the sail to.

Jacob's ladder.—Ropes fitted with wooden rungs from the crosstrees to the top-gallant mast head.

Jam.—A ship is jammed in the wind when she is squeezed close up into it so as to lay half her upper canvas aback. A rope is jammed when it will not haul over a sheave.

Jambs.—Cabin doorposts, &c.

Jaw.—The hollowed end of a gaff. "Give us none of your jaw," no impudence.

Jawing-tackle.—Capacity of talking.

Jawing-tacks.—A speaker is said to have his jawing-tacks aboard when be talks rapidly and at length.

Jaw-rope.—A rope over the jaw of a gaff, to keep it from leaving the mast.

Jaws.—A semicircle at the end of a boom or gaff, to keep it to the mast.

Jeer-block.—A block used in sending a lower yard up or down.

Jeer-capstan.—Formerly the name of a capstan between the fore and main-masts.

Jeers.—Jeers were an assemblage of tackles which, in the days when the lower yards came on deck, were used to hoist and lower them.

Jemmy Ducks.—In a man-of-war the ship's poulterer.

Jemmy-Jessamy.—Dandified. "A jemmy-jessamy sort of fellow," one who gives himself fine airs.

Jersey.—A woollen shirt or overall.

Jet-propeller.—A form of marine propulsion for forcing a vessel along by the ejection of columns of water.

Jetsam.—Goods thrown overboard for preservation of a ship in danger.

Jettison.—The throwing over of goods from a ship for her preservation in a time of danger.

Jewel-block.—A block at the topsail and topgallant yard-arms for the studding-sail halliards to reeve through.

Jib.—A fore-and-aft sail. In large ships there are generally three jibs: the *outer* and *inner* jibs, which set on stays on the jib boom; and the outermost jib, called the *flying-jib*, that sets on a stay on the flying-jib boom.

Jibber the ribber.—A wrecker's trick of luring a ship to destruction by showing a false light.

Jib boom.—A spar supported by the bowsprit and extending beyond it.

Jibguys.—Ropes which support the jib boom sideways.

Jib-header.—The name for a gaff-topsail, shaped like a jib, used in yachts.

Jibing.—When the wind gets on the lee side of a fore-and-aft sail, and blows it over.

Jib of jibs.—A jib that corresponds with a "star-gazer," being indeed an impossible jib.

Jib-topsail.—A small jib that is set above the jib of a yacht.

Jib-traveller.—A ring that travels on the jib boom for the tack of the jib.

Jigger.—The watch-tackle, or Handy Billy. Also a small pump formerly used for feloniously abstracting liquor from casks.

Jiggered.—Jiggered up, I'm used up. "Well, I'm jiggered" seems to be an expression of astonishment.

Jigger-mast.—The lower and last square-rigged mast on a four-masted vessel.

Jigger-topgallant mast and royal mast.—The masts above the jigger-topmast.

Jigger-topgallant sail and royal.—The sails above the jigger-topsail.

Jigger-topmast.—The mast above the jigger lower mast.

Jigger-topsail.—The sail bent to the jigger-topsail yard.

Jigg up!—A cry raised when a jigger-tackle is ready for hauling upon.

Jimmy Green.—A sail that sets on a jib-boom guy.

Job.—A task; work to be done.

Jobation.—A lecture.

Johnny Haultaut.—Merchant-sailor's name for a man-of-war's-man.

Johnny Raw.—A greenhorn.

Jolly.—A marine.

Jolly-boat.—A ship's boat, formerly so called.

Jolly-jumpers.—Light sails set above sky-scrapers, &c.

Jumper.—A frock made of duck or fine canvas.

Jumper-braces.—Ropes for guying down the sprit-sail gaffs to an angle with the horizon when at sea.

Jumping.—A practice on board colliers discharging. It is performed by four men holding whip-lines attached to a rope rove through a block. At the end of the rope is a basket which when filled the men hoist up by jumping backwards off a kind of platform.

Jump-jointed.—Iron plates laid flush or smooth upon a ship's side.

Junk.—Condemned rope unlaid; also salt beef.

Jury-mast.—A temporary mast to replace one that has been lost.

Jury-rudder.—A temporary contrivance for steering a ship when her rudder is lost.

K

Kat.—A timber vessel.

Kanakas.—Natives of the South Sea Islands.

Keckling.—Rope wound round the long ends left in splicing the eye in a rope cable, the ends having been wormed into the lays of the cable.

Kedge.—A small anchor.

Kedging.—Using the kedge anchor to warp the ship by.

Keel.—The lowest and principal timber of a wooden vessel. In iron ships there are several kinds of keel, such as flat-plate keel, bar keel, bilge keel, &c. Also the name of a species of barge or lighter on the rivers Tyne and Wear. A keel of coals is twenty-one tons, five cwts.

Keeleg.—"Up keeleg" means up anchor.

Keel-haul.—An ancient punishment that consisted in dragging a man under a vessel's bottom.

Keelman.—One who works a Newcastle keel.

Keelson.—An internal keel lying fore and aft upon the main keel.

Keel-stroke.—The curvature of the keel forward.

Keep away!—To put the helm up in a squall, so as to run before it.

Keep off.—To keep away.

Keep your luff!—An order to the helmsman to keep the ship close to the wind.

"Keep the compass afloat."—Twitching a compass-bowl to remedy the sluggishness of the card.

Keep your weather eye lifting!—Keep a bright look-out.

Kenning-glass.—Old name for a telescope.

Kentledge.—Pieces of iron for ballast.

Ketch.—A vessel rigged with a little gaff mizzen, like a yawl.

Kettle-bottom.—A flat-floored ship.

Kettle-net.—A mackerel net.

Kevel.—A strong piece of wood used as a cleat for a heavy strain.

Kevel-heads.—Tops of timbers above the deck, used for belaying ropes to.

Key.—A long wharf.

Key or **cay.**—A Bermudan or West Indian coral shoal.

Key model.—The model of a proposed ship.

Kick the bucket.—To die.

Kid.—A kind of tub in which the crew's dinner is placed and taken into the forecastle.

Kid or **cod.**—To joke, to deceive by joking misrepresentations.

Kingston's valves.—Conical valves to close the apertures in a ship's side in case of accident to blow-off cocks, &c.

Kink.—A twist in a rope.

Kippering.—A mode of curing fish.

Kit.—A sailor's wardrobe.

Knees.—Projections on each side the hounds, for the support of the forepart of the trestle-trees.

Knight-heads.—Timbers next to the stem, the ends of them come up through the deck and form a support for the bowsprit.

Knock off!—Desist, stop; also to give up, as "To knock off the sea."

Knock-toe.—A galley-punt (which see).

Knot.—A sea-mile of 2027 yards.

Knots.—The ends of ropes variously twisted, such as single wall, single wall crowned, double wall, Matthew Walker, diamond knot, stopper knot, shroud knot, Turk's head, &c.

Knuckle.—An angle in a timber.

L

L.—The three L's are lead, latitude, and look-out. The look-out probably includes the fourth L, which should be lights.

Labour.—A vessel labours when she strains, wallows, rolls heavily.

Lacing.—Line with which a jib or stay-sail is bent to a stay.

Lady's hole.—Formerly in men-of-war a place where the gunner's small stores were kept. The man appointed to look after those stores was called a "lady."

Lady's ladder.—Said when the ratlins on shrouds are placed too close to one another.

Lagan.—Goods sunk in the sea.

Laid up.—The situation of a vessel when dismantled and not in use.

Lairs.—Dock accommodation for cattle.

Lambusting.—A rope's-ending.

Land-blink.—A brightness of the atmosphere seen on approaching snow-covered land.

Land-breeze.—An off-shore wind.

Land-fall.—Making land when at sea.

Land ho!—The exclamation when land is first sighted.

Landing.—The edge of a plate, in an iron ship, where it overlaps another.

Land-mark.—A shore sign, such as a windmill or church spire, to direct a navigator in steering his ship.

Land-sharks.—Boarding-house keepers, runners, crimps, and all such people as prey upon sailors.

Landsmen.—The old rating of boys or ordinary seamen on their first voyage.

Land-tacks.—"Take to his land-tacks," said of a sailor when he goes ashore for a frisk.

Laniard.—A piece of line to sling or hold anything by. A small rope used to set up rigging with.

Lap.—A term used when the slide valve of a marine engine is at its middle position.

Lap of valve.—The projection of a portion of the slide valve to regulate the admission of steam into the cylinder of an engine.

Larboard.—The term formerly used for the port or left-hand side of a ship.

Larbowlines.—The name formerly given to the port watch.

Lash.—To secure with a line or rope.

Lashing-eye.—A loop for a lashing to reeve through.

Latchings.—The eyes in the head-rope of a bonnet for lacing it. (See Bonnet.)

Lateen.—A triangular sail.

Latitude.—The latitude of a place is its distance from the equator, measured by an arch of meridian.

Latitude in.—The latitude at which a ship arrives.

Latitude left.—The latitude from which a ship has departed.

Launch.—A ship's boat. *To launch* is to liberate a vessel into the sea.

Launch-carronade.—A twelve pound gun formerly carried in a man-of-war's launch.

Launch ho!—Signifying "no higher."

Launching-ways.—Beds of timber on which a vessel slides in a cradle when launched.

Lay.—To come or go. *Lay down—lay aft—lay forward—lay aloft.* The *lay* of a rope is the direction in which the strands are twisted.

Lay.—Whalemen are paid "by the lay," i.e. they have a share in the proceeds of the catches.

Lay along.—"She lay very much along," an old-fashioned phrase signifying that the ship was pressed heavily over on to her broadside by the force of the wind.

Lay-days.—Days specified in a charter-party for loading and discharging.

Lay in!—An order to men to come off a yard.

Laying top.—A piece of wood used in rope-making.

Lay out!—An order to men to make their way along a yard towards the ends. Also, to lay out a warp is to carry it in a boat to a distance from the ship to which one end is attached.

Lazarette.—A space in the after end of a ship in which provisions, stores, &c., are kept.

Lead.—A term used when the piston of a marine engine is at the end of the stroke.

Lead.—The lead of a rope is the direction it takes, rove or other wise, said only of running-gear.

Leading-block.—A block for directing a tackle.

Leading column.—The headmost column of the ships of a fleet.

Leading part.—The part of a tackle that is pulled when the tackle wants overhauling.

Lead line.—A line attached to a leaden weight and used for ascertaining the depth of water. The *hand-line* is from twenty to twenty-five fathoms long; the *deep-sea lead-line* from 100 to 200 fathoms.

Leak.—A hole, an aperture, a rift in a ship that allows the water to penetrate into her.

Leakage.—Loss of liquid cargo by the leaking of it.

Leave.—Permission to be absent.

Leave-breaking.—Not being back within the time required.

Ledges.—Pieces of timber in the framing of the deck let into the carlings for supports.

Lee-board.—A large board at the side of a flat-bottomed vessel to prevent her driving to leeward when on a wind.

Leech.—Side of a sail.

Leech-line.—A rope to haul up the leech of a sail to the yard.

Leech-rope.—That part of the bolt-rope to which the side of a sail is attached.

Lee fang.—A rope for hauling in a fore-and-aft sail, rove through a cringle.

Lee fange.—An iron bar on which the sheets of a fore-and-aft sail travel.

Lee side.—The side opposite that against which the wind blows.

Lee-tide.—A tide that sets the ship to leeward.

Leeward.—Towards the lee side, on the lee side.

Leeward ebb.—When the wind and tide are both setting out.

Leeward flood.—When the wind and tide are both setting in.

Leewardly.—Said of a vessel that drifts with the wind.

Lee way.—The drift a ship makes when sailing near the wind.

Lee wheel.—The lee side of the helm, applied to the helmsman who holds the lee spokes.

Leg.—A board or run on a single tack.

Legs.—She has legs, said of a fast ship.

Lend a hand!—A call for help in hauling, &c.

Length between perpendiculars.—The length of a vessel, measured on her main deck, from the fore side of stem to the after side of sternpost.

Let draw!—The order to let the jibs go over to leeward in tacking.

Let fall!—The order to drop a sail when the gaskets are cast adrift.

Let fly!—An order to let go a rope quickly.

Let go and haul!—An order in tacking to swing the fore-yards and brace them up.

Letter of marque.—A privately-owned vessel furnished with a commission empowering her to make reprisals on enemy's ships.

Levanter.—A strong Mediterranean wind.

Levelling-blocks.—Massive plates used in iron ship-building for bending the frames.

Liberty.—Leave of absence.

Liberty-men.—Those of a crew who have a holiday ashore.

Liberty-pole.—The fore-mast.

Lieutenant.—A commissioned officer next in rank under a commander.

Life-line.—Any line stretched along to prevent men from being washed away.

Lifting propeller.—A propeller that can be raised or lowered to prevent the engines from "racing" (see also "race"). The absence of a keel-piece between the inner and outer sternposts enables the propeller to be depressed until the lower part of it is beneath the keel.

Lifting sail.—A sail whose tendency is to raise the bows out of water—such as a jib or square fore-sail .

Lifts.—Ropes to support the yard-arms and leading thence to the mast-head.

Light.—To haul over. *Light out,* haul out, or haul over.

Light.—Said of a ship in ballast.

Light dues.—Dues levied on ships passing and benefiting from lights, beacons, buoys, &c.

Lighter.—A large boat for the conveyance of cargo.

Lighterman.—One who conveys goods in a lighter.

Lighthouses.—The legal definition includes floating and other lights exhibited for the guidance of ships.

Light-port.—An aperture for showing a light through.

Light-room.—A compartment furnished with windows for the safe transmission of light to enable the gunner to handle the ammunition, &c.

Lights.—Lamps to be carried at night by vessels to indicate their character, &c.

A *steamer* carries a bright light at the fore-mast, a red light on the port side, a green light on the starboard side.

A *sailing ship* carries a red light on the port side and a green light on the starboard side.

A *steam* or *sailing ship* at anchor shows a single white light.

A *pilot vessel* carries a white light at the mast-head.

Light-ship.—A vessel with a mast-head light or lights, anchored near sands, shoals, &c.

Lightsman.—One of the crew of a light-ship.

Limber boards or **plates.**—Coverings to the limbers to keep dirt out of them.

Limber-clearer.—A chain passed through the limber-passage for clearing it.

Limbers.—Gutters formed on each side of the keelson to allow the water to pass to the pump-well.

Limber-strakes.—The first band of inside plank from the keelson.

Lime-juicer.—Nickname given by Americans to British ships and sailors on account of the lime-juice served out in our Mercantile Marine.

Limmer.—A side rope for a ladder or steps.

Line.—The sailor's name for the equator.

Line abreast.—Ships of a column ranged in line abeam of each other.

Line ahead.—A term in fleet manoeuvres applied to a column when its ships are in one line ahead of each other.

Line-of-battle ships.—Before the days of ironclads ships of seventy-four guns and upwards.

Liner.—A line-of-battle ship. Also, one of a line of ocean-going ships.

Line-tub.—A tub in a whale-boat to coil up the line used in whaling.

Lingo.—Sailor's name for a language he does not understand.

Lining.—The inside planking of a ship.

List.—The inclination of a vessel to port or starboard through bad stowage of cargo or other causes.

Live-lumber.—Passengers, cattle, &c.

Lively.—Buoyant in a seaway.

Liverpool button.—The name for a kind of toggle used by sailors when they lose a button off their coats.

Live stock.—The pigs, sheep, poultry, &c., tarried by a ship to kill for provisions during the voyage.

Living gale.—A tremendous gale.

Lizard.—A piece of rope fitted with an iron eye or thimble for ropes to lead through; it has sometimes two legs.

Lloyd's agents.—Persons appointed at ports for the protection of the interests of insurers of ships.

Lloyd's Registry.—A community of shipowners and others who publish a register in which, on payment of fees, they enter particulars of ships. They appoint surveyors to inspect and grant certificates to ships.

Loaded factors.—Calculations expressed in figures for loading ships to ensure a certain height of side or freeboard.

Load-line.—A mark on each side of a merchant vessel to indicate the line of immersion in salt water to which the owner intends to load the ship for the voyage.

Loblolly boy.—Old name for sick-berth attendant.

Lobscouse.—A mess consisting of meat, biscuit, slush, &c., baked.

Local attraction.—The influence of iron or steel in the neighbourhood of the compass upon the needle, called *aberration of the needle.*

Locker.—A fixed long box used as a seat; a place to stow things away in, such as chain-locker, where the cables are kept.

Log.—A salt water mud worm. Also the apparatus for showing speed

Log-book.—A journal kept by the mate relating to the weather, winds, courses, &c.

Logged.—A man is said to have been logged when his name is entered in the official log-book for insubordination, &c.

Loggerhead.—A sort of post fitted to a whaling-boat's bottom and rising about two feet above the level of the stern platform.

Log-line.—A line wound on a reel. At the end of the line is a piece of wood with a peg in it called a logship. On the logship being thrown overboard the velocity with which the vessel leaves it astern is measured by a second-glass.

Log-minutes.—Entries in a log-book.

Log-ship.—A piece of wood or canvas bag at the end of a log-line for catching the water whilst the log is being hove.

Log-slate.—A slate on which the officer of the watch writes down particulars to be afterwards copied into the log-book.

Long-balls.—Shot fired from a long distance.

Long-boat.—A ship's boat usually carried forward of amidships in sailing vessels.

Longers.—The name given to the longest of a freight of casks.

Longitude.—The longitude of a place is an arch of the equator between the first meridian and that which passes through the place.

Longitude in.—The longitude at which a ship arrives.

Longitude left.—The longitude from which a ship has departed.

Long legs.—Long tacks.

Long lizard.—A pendant for carrying the lower boom topping-lift out to the fore-yard-arm.

Long shoreman.—Literally, one who lives along the shore, such as boatmen, watermen, &c. It is a term of contempt often applied to a sailor.

Long splice.—A connexion formed by unlaying a length of the strands of two ropes, laying up one strand in the room of another, and dividing and knotting.

Long stay.—When the cable forms a small angle with the ground, owing to the anchor being some distance ahead.

Long-togs.—Clothes worn ashore.

Long topgallant mast.—A topgallant mast, royal mast, and sky-sail mast all in one.

Loof.—A term to indicate the beginning of the curve of the planks as they approach the stern. Also, the old term for the after part of the bows of a ship.

Look-out.—The man stationed to look out for whatever he can see.

Loom.—An enlarged appearance, due to fog or darkness. Also, the part of an oar that is in a boat when the rest of it is out. *To loom* is to show up large.

Loose-fish.—A whaling term signifying that the whale is fair game for anybody who can catch it.

Loovered boards.—A kind of venetian blinds over a ship's ports.

Lowdah.—A Chinese sailing-master.

Lower away!—Lower an object down.

Lower cheek.—A knee bolted to the bows of the ship and knee of the head.

Lower counter-rail.—A projected moulding on the stern of a ship.

Lower deckers.—Guns on the lower deck.

Lower fore-topgallant sail.—The under portion of a double topgallant sail whose clews are stretched upon the topsail yard.

Lower fore-topsail.—The under portion of the fore-topsail whose clews are stretched upon the fore-yard.

Lower main-topsail.—The under portion of the top-sail, whose clews are stretched upon the main-yard.

Lower mizzen-topsail.—The under portion of the top-sail whose clews are stretched upon the crossjack yard.

Lower studding-sail.—A large square sail extended beyond the fore-yard by the fore-topmast studding-sail boom and the swinging boom.

Lower studding-sail tripping-line.—A line leading through a thimble in the middle of the lower studding-sail and bent to the tack for taking it in.

Lower yardmen.—Men whose duty it is to furl or reef the courses.

Low pressure.—A method of disposing of used-up steam by passing it into the condenser through the eduction pipe and converting it into water.

Lubber's hole.—An aperture in the tops so called because raw hands prefer to creep through it to going over the futtock shrouds.

Lubber's point.—A mark on the compass bowl in a line with the ship's head for the helmsman to keep the course to.

Luff.—A naval lieutenant. Also the weather side of a fore-and-aft sail. *To luff* is to bring a ship closer to the wind.

Luff-tackle.—A tackle consisting of a double and a single block, each fitted with a hook.

Luff upon luff.—A luff-tackle hooked to the fall of another luff-tackle, thus increasing the purchase.

Lugger.—A vessel rigged with a lug-sail. She has two or three masts. Some luggers carry top-sails.

Lugsail.—A sail shaped somewhat square and hoisted by a yard.

Lump.—A lighter.

Lumpers.—Men employed in taking in and discharging cargo.

Lunar day.—The interval between the moon's departure from, and return to, the same meridian.

Lunar observation.—The measurement of the angular distance between the moon and sun, or between the moon and certain stars or planets.

Lunars.—Lunar observations: a method of obtaining the mean time of the day or night from the observed altitude of a celestial body, and comparing it with the mean solar time at Greenwich as shown by chronometer.

Lurch.—The sudden heavy roll of a ship on one side.

Lush.—Drink.

Lying along.—The situation of a ship pressed down by a gale.

M

Made mast.—A mast made of several pieces.

Magazines.—Powder-rooms in a man-of-war, called the fore and aft magazines.

Magnetic axis.—The direction of the magnetism of the needle.

Magnetic course.—A compass course corrected for deviation and leeway. Or the angle that a ship's track makes with the magnetic meridian.

Main bowline.—A bowline that hauls out the weather leech of the main-sail.

Main-hatch.—The aperture in the deck through which the main-hold is entered.

Main-hold.—The central portion of the hold.

Main-mast.—The middle lower mast of a ship.

Main-royal backstay.—A support leading from the head of the royal mast.

Main-royal mast.—The mast above the main-topgallant mast.

Main-royal stay.—A support leading forward from the head of the royal mast to the head of the fore-topmast.

Main-royal staysail.—A fore-and-aft sail that sets on a stay from the main-royal mast-head to the head of the fore-topmast.

Main-royal yard.—The yard above the topgallant yard.

Main-sail.—In a ship the sail that is bent to the main-yard. In a schooner the sail that is extended by a gaff and boom on the main-mast. A *boom main-sail* is a main-sail the foot of which is extended upon a boom. This term is sometimes given to a brig's try-sail.

Main-sail haul!—The order to swing the main and mizzen yards in tacking.

Main sheet.—The ropes by which the lee lower corner of the main-sail is hauled aft.

Main-skysail mast.—The mast above the main-royal mast.

Main-skysail.—A fore-and-aft sail that sets on a stay between the fore and main masts.

Main-stay.—A support leading from the head of the main-mast to the deck.

Main-tack.—The ropes which keep down the weather lower corner of the main-sail.

Main tackle.—A tackle used in securing the mast, setting up rigging, &c.

Main-top bowline.—The bowline for hauling out the weather leech of the main-topsail.

Main-topgallant.—In former times a flag was always said, when hoisted at the mast-head, to be flown at the main-topgallant, because in those days ships did not carry royal masts.

Main-topgallant backstay.—A support leading from the head of the topgallant mast.

Main-topgallant mast.—The mast above the main-topmast.

Main-topgallant stay.—A support leading forward from the head of the main-topgallant mast to the head of the fore-mast.

Main-topgallant staysail.—A fore-and-aft sail that sets on a stay from the topgallant mast-head to the head of the foremast.

Main-topgallant yard.—The yard above the topsail yards.

Main-topmast.—The mast above the main-mast.

Main-topmast backstay.—A support leading from the head of the top-mast to the side of the ship.

Main-topmast stay.—A support leading forward from the head of the top-mast to the deck.

Main-topmast staysail.—A fore-and-aft sail that sets on a stay from the top-mast head.

Main-topsail yards.—Double yards next above the main-yard.

Main wales.—Lower wales into which the maindeck knee-bolts come.

Main-yard.—The lowest yard on the main-mast.

Main-yard men.—Men on the sick list.

Make.—To descry, as to make land. Also to approach, as the tide makes.

Make bad weather.—Said of a ship that rolls heavily and takes in water on deck.

Make eight bells!—The order to strike the bell eight times, signifying that it is noon by the sun.

Make headway.—The direct way a ship makes in sailing or steaming

Making bad weather.—Said of a vessel labouring heavily, shipping quantities of water, &c.

Make sail.—To add to the canvas already set.

Make water.—To leak.

Mallet.—A small wooden hammer

Man.—To man is to furnish a ship or boat with a crew.

Managing owner.—One of a firm who superintends or looks after all the business of a ship, and whose name is registered at the custom house of the ship's port of registry.

Manger.—A kind of shelf in a man-of-war's bows behind the hawse holes, with a coaming and scupper holes, meant to receive and eject the water when the cables are bent.

Manhandled.—Rudely handled by men. Moved by their force of muscle.

Manhole.—An aperture to enable a man to enter a marine boiler to clean it.

Manifest.—A document containing ship's name, port of registry, registered tonnage, particulars of cargo, port of loading and discharge, list of passengers, stores, crew, &c., signed by the master.

Manoeuvring.—Working a ship by her sails.

Man-of-war fashion.—Said of a merchant-ship in smart order, with a good crew, &c.

Manometer.—A steam-gauge.

Man-ropes.—Lines over the side of a ship to hold by in mounting or descending the steps.

Man the windlass!—The order to get the anchor up.

Mares' tails.—Feather-like clouds indicative of wind.

Marine.—The navy or the merchant service. Also a man belonging to the troops employed in the navy.

Marine.—An empty bottle. Sometimes called dead marine or marine officer.

Marine Boards.—Local Marine Boards were appointed to carry out the provisions of the Merchant Shipping Acts.

Marine glue.—A glutinous, adhesive substance used in ship-building.

Mariner.—A sailor.

Mariner's compass.—An instrument for steering ships. It consists of three principal parts—the card, the needle on its lower surface, and the case.

Marine stores.—The ropes, sails, provisions, &c, of a ship.

Marks.—Depths marked on the band lead-line; i.e. 3, 5, 7, 10, 13, 15, 17 and 20 fathoms. The marks between are called *deeps*. Thus "by the mark 7" means seven fathoms, "by the deep 9" means nine fathoms. The fractions are a half and a quarter. 5½ fathoms are called "and a half five," 5¾ fathoms are called "a quarter less six."

Marl.—To wind rope or small stuff round a rope.

Marline.—Two-stranded small stuff.

Marline-spike.—A bar of tapering iron with an eye at the thick end, used for opening the strands of rope for splicing, &c.

Marling-hitch.—A knot used in the process of marling.

Maroon.—To maroon a man is to set him ashore on a desolate coast or island.

Marooned.—Set ashore alone on a desert island or coast.

Marry.—To join ropes together with a worming.

Martingale.—A spar under the bowsprit end, used for guying down the headstays.

Martnets.—Leechlines.

Massoolah boats.—Madras surf-boats.

Mast carlings.—Timbers which frame the partners.

Mast coat.—Canvas fitted round the mast, where it penetrates the upper deck, to prevent water from draining through the aperture.

Master.—The captain of a merchant ship.

Master mariner.—One who holds a certificate from the Board of Trade, showing that he has passed his examination as a master mariner. The master of a merchant-vessel.

Mast-head.—The portion of the mast from the eyes of the rigging to the top of the mast.

Mastheading.—Sending a midshipman aloft as a punishment.

Mast-head men.—Look-out men aloft.

Mast-partners.—A framing of timber between the beams for the support of masts.

Mate.—Signifies chief mate. There are 2nd, 3rd, 4th, and even 5th mates. The chief mate is the officer next in rank to the captain. He heads the port watch. The term also signifies an assistant, such as cook's mate, boatswain's mate, carpenter's mate, &c.

Mats.—Made of old unlaid rope and used as chafing gear.

Maul.—A large iron hammer used by shipwrights.

Meaking iron.—A caulker's tool for extracting oakum from seams.

Measured mile.—A nautical mile for testing speeds of steamers.

Medical inspector.—An inspector appointed by the Board of Trade or a local Marine Board to inspect, on application, any seaman applying for employment on board a ship.

Medico.—Ship's doctor.

Meet her when she shakes!—The order to shift the helm when a vessel rounds into the wind.

Mercantile Marine Fund.—A fund created by fees, light-dues, ballastage rates, &c., and chargeable with salaries and expenses in connexion with marine boards, lighting the coasts, lifeboats, and other expenses.

Mercator's chart or projection.—A chart on which the meridians are drawn parallel to one another, the meridional degrees being increased between the parallels, so that the proportion between a degree of latitude and longitude may be everywhere preserved on the chart.

Mercator's sailing.—The art of finding on a plane chart the progress of a ship along a given course.

Merchantman.—A passenger or cargo vessel.

Mess.—The division of the crew, or the officers who eat together.

Messenger.—A rope or chain for heaving in the cable.

Metacentre.—Sir. E. J. Reed defines this word thus:—"As regards the 'metacentre,' I must explain that in former times, when 'initial stability' alone was calculated, the word 'metacentre' had a much more limited meaning than it possesses now. It formerly had relation to the upright position of the vessel, in which case the buoyancy acts upwards through the centre line of the ship's course. After receiving a slight inclination the vessel has, as we have said, a new centre of buoyancy, and the buoyancy itself will act upwards along a fresh line slightly inclined to what was previously the upright line. This point was called the 'metacentre.' It is shown that when a ship is much more inclined, the point at which two consecutive lines of the buoyancy's upward action will intersect may not be and often will not be in the middle line of the ship at all, but this point is nevertheless called the 'metacentre,' and the use of the word in this extended sense has recently become general."

Metacentric height.—A delusive method of calculating a ship's stability by computations which fix the metacentric height between points based upon the submerged volume of the hull, the weight of the machinery, freight, equipment, &c.

Metage.—Charges for weighing cargo.

Microscope.—A small lens for reading off the divisions on the graduated limb and vernier of a sextant.

Middle latitude sailing.—A method of navigating a ship, compounded of plane and parallel sailing.

Middle timber.—The central timber in the stern.

Middle watch.—The watch from midnight till four in the morning.

"Midge" system.—A system instituted by the Board of Trade for authorized persons to board all ships entering the port of London and induce the sailor to have his money forwarded to whatever part he is going to, in order to anticipate the harpies who prey upon seamen. "Midge" was the name of the steamer employed for the purpose of boarding.

Midshipman.—A naval cadet. In the merchant service a youth who does boy's work for which privilege his friends pay the owners of the vessel.

Midshipman's nuts.—Pieces of biscuit.

Mincer.—The name given to the sailor aboard a whaleman, whose duty it is to mince the horse-pieces of blubber for the try-pots.

Minion.—An old piece of ordnance used in ships; it threw a 4 lb. shot.

Minute-guns.—Guns fired every minute at a funeral.

Miss stays.—To fail in tacking.

Mitch board.—A crutch to support a mast when lowered.

Mits.—Rude gloves worn by sailors in very cold weather.

Mizzen.—A large fore-and-aft sail on the mizzen-mast of a ship or barque. Also called spanker.

Mizzen boom.—A small spar at the foot of a yawl's mizzen.

Mizzen-mast.—The aftermost lower mast.

Mizzen-royal mast.—The mast above the mizzen-topgallant mast.

Mizzen-royal yard.—The yard above the topgallant yard.

Mizzen-topgallant mast.—The mast above the mizzen-topmast.

Mizzen-topgallant staysail.—A fore-and-aft sail that sets on a stay from the topgallant mast-head to the head of the mainmast.

Mizzen-topgallant yard.—The yard above the topsail yards.

Mizzen-topmast.—The mast above the mizzen lower mast.

Mizzen-topmast staysail.—A fore-and-aft sail that sets on a stay, from the topmast head to the main-mast.

Mizzen-topsail yards.—The yards above the crossjack yard.

Mocking system.—A term applied to the method of building small vessels by bending battens to the stem, sternpost, and keel without *laying off*.

Monitor.—Armoured steamer, of small draught, with one or more revolving turrets furnished with large guns. An American term.

Monkey.—An iron sliding ram used in driving in armour bolts in ironclads.

Monkey-block.—A small single block stropped with a swivel.

Monkey-poop.—This name has been given to a platform connecting a fore and after cabin in the after part of a vessel. It may also signify a very short poop.

Monkey-pump.—A pipe-stem or straw for sucking the contents of a cask.

Monkey-sparred.—Said of a ship when under-rigged.

Monsoons.—Trade-winds in the Indian Ocean.

Moon-blink.—Blindness caused by sleeping in the moonlight.

Mooney.—Partially intoxicated.

Moon-rakers.—Small sails above the sky-sails.

Moon-sail.—A sail above the sky-sail.

Moon-sheered.—Said of a ship with high upper works.

Moor.—A ship is moored when she has two anchors down in different directions.

Mooring-board.—A device to enable a ship moored and belonging to a fleet to ascertain the bearing and distance of either of her anchors from a given point.

Mooring-pipes.—Apertures in a steamer's side for leading ropes for mooring purposes.

Moorings.—Buoys to which vessels are fastened.

Mooring-swivel.—A swivel to prevent a ship from getting a foul hawse when moored.

Moorsom's rule.—A method of ascertaining the internal capacity of a ship by expressing it in cubic feet, and dividing by 100, each 100 feet to be a ton.

Morning gun.—A gun fired to announce daybreak.

Morning watch.—The watch from four a.m. till eight a.m.

Mortar.—A gun to throw life-lines to vessels in distress.

Morticed-block.—A single block of wood hollowed to receive a sheave.

Mortices.—Square holes in the trawl-heads used by smacks for the trawl-beam to fit into.

Moulding-book.—A manuscript book containing information relative to the mouldings of timbers, &c., used in some shipyards.

Moulds.—The patterns of a vessel's frames.

Mouse-lines.—Lines stretched over a ship in a dock to suspend a plummet to. They are intended to point out the centre of the docking blocks.

Mousing.—Small stuff wound round a hook to prevent it from slipping.

Mowree.—A New Zealander.

Mudhole.—An aperture near the bottom of a marine boiler for removing the deposit of mud and scale.

Mudlarks.—Formerly a name given to river thieves.

Mud pilot.—A pilot who carries a ship between the Docks of London and Gravesend.

Muffle.—To muffle oars is to put mats or canvas round the part that rests in the rowlock or between the thole-pins.

Munions.—The pieces between the lights in the galleries of ships in former times.

Muntz's metal.—A combination of metals used for sheathing a vessel's bottom.

Murdering-pieces.—An old name for cannons which were mounted upon the after part of the forecastle, with their muzzles greatly elevated.

Muster.—To muster the watch is to call over their names, each man answering, that it may be known all are on deck. In the same way the crew is mustered.

N

Nadir.—The nadir of a place is a point in the heavens immediately under it.

Name board.—A board affixed to the bows of a vessel on which her name is written.

National ship.—A state ship, a ship of war, a public ship.

Nautical Almanack.—An important and valuable work, full of calculations, and essential to the navigator.

Nautical Assessor.—A retired shipmaster or naval officer appointed to assist magistrates and justices of the peace in deciding upon marine questions.

Nautical mile.—6080 feet.

Naval armament.—Ships of war fitted out for a particular service.

Naval court.—A court composed of three to five members, consisting of a naval officer not below the rank of lieutenant, a consular officer, a master of a British merchantman, and the others, British merchants, ship-masters or naval officers.

Naval hoods.—Planking above and below the hawse-holes.

Naval lines.—Lines for holding truss-pendants parallel, that they may render more easily.

Naval officer.—One belonging to the Royal Navy.

Naval Reserve.—Merchant seamen who have volunteered to serve in the Royal Navy in war time. They are paid a trifling sum per year and are entitled to a pension.

Nave-hole.—A hole in a gun-truck for the axle-tree.

Navigable.—Said of a channel or river capable of being navigated.

Navigation.—The art of conducting a ship through the sea from one place to another. It is divided into two branches, *Seamanship*, comprehending the knowledge of the sails, rigging, steering, &c., and *Navigation Proper*, that is, the finding the ship's latitude and longitude with the sextant, &c.

Navigation laws.—Protective laws framed with the idea of promoting the interests of British shipping and British seamen. Long since repealed.

Navigator.—One who can steer his ship by the art of navigation, but not necessarily a seaman.

Neaped.—Stranded by a spring tide, and having to wait for the next spring tide to float.

Neap tides.—Low tides coincident with the moon's second and fourth quarters.

Near.—Close to the wind.

Necked.—Said of a treenail when bent or cracked in the timbers of a ship.

Necking.—A moulding on the taffrail.

Necklace.—A rope or chain with legs fitted round the mast-head and used for making hanging blocks for the jib, stay-sail and stay, fast to.

Negative slip.—The neutralization of a certain amount of the propulsion of the screw of a steam-ship, due to the water dragged after her in her wake.

Nettings.—Where the hammocks in men-of-war are stowed, fitted round the ship on top of the bulwarks.

Nettles.—The halves of yarns in the unlaid end of a rope twisted up for pointing or grafting.

Net tonnage.—In sailing ships, the deduction from the gross tonnage of the tonnage of space appropriated to the use of crews. In steamers, in addition to the deduction of crew space, the gross tonnage is further reduced by an allowance for spaces occupied by the propelling power.

Neutral bottom.—A ship that in war-time takes no part with the belligerents.

Newcome.—A fresh hand just arrived.

News.—"Do you hear the news?" an exclamation that sometimes follows the call to the watch below to turn out.

Ninepin block.—A block shaped like a ninepin, and used as a fair-leader.

Nip.—A short turn in a rope.

Nipcheese.—The old name for the purser's steward.

Nippering.—Securing nippers by cross turns to jam them.

Nippers.—Marled yarns for binding the messenger to the cable and used for various purposes.

N.M.—New measurement. A method of ascertaining the internal cubical contents of a ship by certain calculations. Enacted in 1854.

Nock.—The upper fore-end of a sail that sets with a boom.

Nog.—A treenail or fastening.

No man's land.—The old name of a space between the belfry and the bows of a boat stowed on the booms.

Nominal horse-power.—A power assumed to equal 33,000 lbs., raised one foot high in one minute.

Norie's Epitome.—The best treatise on navigation ever published.

Non-return valve.—A valve in connexion with the feed-cock of a marine boiler, to prevent the return of the water from the boiler.

Nous.—Used at sea as a synonym for spunk.

Norman.—A wooden bar or iron pin.

Nose.—The stem of a ship.

Notaries public.—Persons authorized to draw up official statements made by a shipmaster, regarding damage, failure of merchants to furnish cargoes, &c.

Nothing off.—An order to the helmsman to keep the vessel close to the wind.

Notions.—A mixed cargo of small things for sale or barter.

Noting protest.—A protest noted by a shipmaster before a public notary, magistrate, or consul, when sea-perils have occurred. It forms the shipowner's defence for non-delivery of goods, or for their delivery in a damaged state. It is also an instrument for the recovery of contributions from persons interested in the safety of the voyage. It also supports the shipowner in his claim upon the underwriters.

Number.—The number of a ship's certificate of registry. Making her number is said of a ship hoisting the flags which indicate her name.

Nun-buoy.—A buoy tapering at each end.

Nurse.—The first lieutenant of a man-of-war commanded by a captain who is there by influence, but who has no capacity.

O

Oakum.—Yarns picked into hemp.

Oar.—A long piece of wood with a blade at one end.

Oars!—The command to stop rowing by raising the oars from the water and letting them lie horizontally in the rowlocks.

Oblique sailing.—A method of navigation adopted in coasting along shores, surveying coasts, &c.

Observation.—To get an observation is to take the altitude of a heavenly body.

Occulting.—A light visible for less than thirty seconds between eclipses.

Odd backstay.—The foremost one, serving as a breast backstay.

Odd shroud.—The after shroud.

Off and on.—Keeping near the land by heading in and standing out.

Officer of the watch.—The lieutenant or mate in charge of the deck.

Official log-book.—A book for special entries, such as sickness, death, desertion, mutiny, drunkenness, &c.

Offing.—Distance from the shore.

Oilskins.—The waterproof coat, leggings, and sou'-wester worn by sailors.

Old man.—The term applied to the captain by a crew.

Old standing rigging makes bad running gear.—Signifying that old seamen will not do for posts requiring activity, and usually filled by young men.

Oldster.—A midshipman or apprentice who has already made one or more voyages.

O.M.—Old measurement, known as Builder's Measurement. This measurement was according to an old law of 1773. The length of the keel was multiplied by the breadth of the vessel measured in a prescribed manner, the product multiplied by half the breadth, and the whole divided by 94. The quotient was considered to give the true contents of the tonnage.

On a bowline.—Close to the wind with the bowline hauled out.

On a wind.—Sailing close to the wind.

On deck there!—A call from up aloft or from the hold for attention.

Only mate.—The only mate carried in a ship. For a steamer, he must be nineteen years of age, and must have served five years at sea, in order to qualify him for an examination for a certificate.

On the beam.—Said of an object right abreast.

On the bow.—Said of an object that bears more or less to the right or left of the bowsprit.

On the quarter.—Said of an object that bears abaft the beam on either hand.

Open hawse.—To ride with two anchors down without a cross in the cables.

Open policy.—A policy of marine insurance, that does not name the values of the interests insured, but leaves them to be ascertained, should a loss happen.

Order-book.—A book for entering the orders of an admiral or senior officer.

Ordinary seaman.—The term applied to a sailor who is rated after and next to Able Seaman.

Orlop.—The deck next the hold of a man-of-war.

O.S.—Initials to signify ordinary seaman.

Oscillating engine.—A marine engine in which the cylinder follows the oscillations of the crank.

Outer jib.—A fore-and-aft sail, setting on a stay, from the fore-topmast-head to the end of the jib-boom.

Outfit.—The stores, gear, furniture, &c., of a ship; a term signifying every requisite for a voyage. Also applied to clothes.

Outhaul.—A rope to haul out the spanker or a try-sail.

Out of gear.—A marine engine is said to be thrown out of gear when the eccentric is detached from the slide valve gear.

Outports.—All ports in Great Britain out of London.

Outrigger.—A boat with rowlocks extended by arms. Also a spar on the crosstrees to spread the royal and top-gallant backstays. Also a log of wood at the side of a boat, to prevent it capsizing. Also a spar to extend leading blocks or the foot of a sail.

Outsail.—A ship is said to outsail another when she beats her in sailing.

Outward desertion.—Desertion of ships outward bound, lying in British ports.

Outwards.—A term signifying that a ship is entered at the Custom House to depart from a home port for a foreign place.

Overboard.—Over the side; out of the ship.

Overfalls.—Casts of the lead showing great unevenness of bottom.

Overhand knot.—The end of a rope passed over the standing part and through the bight.

Overhaul.—Variously used. *Overhaul a clewline*, ease it up; *overhaul a tackle*, pull on the leading parts so as to lengthen the interval between the blocks. Again, to overhaul is to examine.

Overhaul the cable.—To ease the bights of the chain cable around the windlass barrel so that it may pay out through the hawse-pipe.

Overloading.—Putting more cargo into a ship than she is safely able to carry in any condition of weather. Simple as the definition of this term appears, there are few words whose meaning has been more disputed. Owners have one definition, sailors another, the Board of Trade a third.

Over-rake.—Waves over-rake a ship when they break over her bows as she rides at anchor.

Over-rigged.—Top-hampered with heavy gear.

Over-sea.—Over-sea vessels are vessels from foreign ports.

Owners.—The proprietors of a ship.

P

Packet.—A mail-boat.

Pack-ice.—Fragments of ice heaped together.

Packing.—Metal rings, hemp, india-rubber, &c., used to render pistons, slide-valves, &c., steam-tight.

Packing-box.—A steam-tight partition in a marine engine.

Pad.—A piece of timber fixed on a beam for the curve of the deck.

Paddle-box boats.—Boats fitted to the paddle-box bottom up.

Paddle-boxes.—Large semi-circular casings for enclosing the upper part of the wheels of a paddle-steamer.

Paddy.—Rice in the husk.

Painter.—A rope in the bow of a boat.

Palm.—The fluke of an anchor. Also a piece of leather with a shape of iron let into it, fitting around the hand and into the palm, and used by sail-makers in sewing canvas.

Pampero.—A squall encountered in the Rio de la Plata.

Paper-boat.—A boat sheathed with very thin planking.

Parallax.—The difference between the true and apparent place of a celestial body; the apparent place being its situation when viewed from the surface of the earth, and the true place its situation if observed at the same time from the centre of the earth.

Parallel motion.—A name applied to a contrivance in an engine by means of which the piston-rod is made to work in a straight line parallel to the inner surface of the cylinder.

Parallel of latitude.—A circle parallel to the equator.

Parallel sailing.—A method of finding the distance between two places in the same latitude when their difference of longitude is known, or of finding the difference of longitude answering to the meridian distance when a ship sails east or west.

Parbuckle.—A rope round a spar or cask for hoisting or lowering.

Parcelling.—Wrapping narrow strips of tarred canvas round a rope.

Parliament-heel.—The situation of a ship laid over by shifting her ballast in order to get at her bottom side.

Parral.—That which confines an upper yard to the mast at the centre.

Part.—To break. "The rope parted," the rope broke.

Particular average.—Damage or partial loss unavoidably happening to an individual interest through peril insured against.

Partners.—Frames of timber to solidify holes in which masts, capstans, bitts, pumps, &c., are sunk.

Pass.—To take turns with a rope or seizing, &c.

Passing-box.—A case formerly used in which powder was handed up for serving a gun.

Patent log.—An instrument of brass, a portion of which rotates in the water, the number of revolutions being expressed by miles on the indexes.

Patent reefing topsail.—A plan by which a top-sail reefs itself by the yard rolling up the sail as it is lowered.

Patent slip.—A slip for hauling up vessels for repairs.

Paul-bitt.—A strong timber fitted with notched iron for checking the reverse action of the windlass by catching the pawls.

Paul-rim.—A notched iron ring let into the deck for the capstan pauls to work in.

Paunch.—A piece of wood formerly affixed to the fore and main-masts of ships to allow the lower yards, in their descent, to pass clear of the mast hoops.

Paunch-mats.—Used for chafing gear.

Pawl over all!—Heaving the windlass round with one continuous motion.

Pawls.—Movable pieces of iron to prevent a capstan, windlass barrel, or winch from slipping backwards.

Pay.—To pay is to cover oakum in caulked seams with melted pitch.

Paying off.—When a ship's head falls from the wind.

Paymaster.—The title of the person who fills the post on board a man-of-war formerly occupied by the purser. He has the charge of provisions, pays the crew, &c.

Pay out.—To pass out rope.

Pazaree.—A rope used for guying the clews of the fore-sail out by reeving it through a block on the swinging boom.

Pea.—The bill of an anchor. See Bill.

Pea-jacket.—A stout pilot-cloth all-round coat.

Peak.—The upper aftermost corner of a spanker or try-sail.

Peak-downhaul.—A rope at the end of the gaff to haul it down by.

Peak-halliards.—A tackle connected with the end of the gaff for hoisting it.

Peak-purchase.—A purchase for tautening standing-peak halliards.

Pennant.—Flown only by ships of war; the English is a long strip of bunting with St. George's cross in the head. Also a rope to which a purchase is hooked.

Percentage of spare buoyancy.—The proportion borne by the part of a ship that is above water, and which part is for the purpose of floating her, to the portion that is under water.

Persuader.—A rope's end, stick, belaying pin, anything a man can be struck with.

Petard.—A metal machine filled with gunpowder, and fired by a pole.

Petty officer.—A divisional seaman in the navy of the first class.

Philadelphia catechism.—The following doggerel is so called,
Six days shalt thou labour, and do all thou art able,
And on the seventh—holystone the decks and scrape the cable.

Philadelphia lawyer.—"Enough to puzzle a"—Jack's growl over a story he cannot wholly disbelieve nor accept.

Picaroon.—A privateersman. Also a piratical vessel.

Piccary.—Small piracies.

Picking up a wind.—To deviate in search of trade or other constant breeze.

Pickling.—Rubbing brine into a sailor's back after a flogging; also a mode of preserving naval timber.

Pick up.—To "pick up a sail" is to raise it on to the yard for stowing.

Pierced.—Pierced for guns means the apertures in a ship's side through which guns can be discharged.

Piercer.—A kind of small marline-spike for making eyelet-holes.

Pierhead jump.—The tumbling of sailors aboard a ship at the last moment from the dock or pierhead.

Pierman.—A man employed by harbour authorities for making fast or letting go warps, fasts, &c., for vessels, and doing other work about a harbour.

Pigs.—Pieces of iron used as ballast.

Pig-tail.—Tobacco for chewing. Sailors generally chew the plug or square.

Pilchard drivers.—Small Cornish smacks, half-decked luggers.

Pillar buoy.—A buoy having a tall central structure on a broad base.

Pillars.—Iron bars riveted to the beams of iron ships, and secured through the deck-plank to the beam below, to increase structural strength.

Pillow.—A block under the inner end of the bowsprit.

Pill yawl.—A Bristol Channel pilot-boat.

Piloting.—Piloting is divided into two branches. Common piloting, which means the knowledge of how to coast along shore, and proper piloting, which means the knowledge of how to navigate a ship by the heavenly bodies when out of sight of land.

Pilots.—Persons licensed by the Trinity House, and by local authorities to navigate ships in certain waters.

Pilot-signals.—A ship requiring a pilot signals as follows: in the day time she hoists the Jack or other national colour worn by merchant ships, at the fore, or a square blue flag, with a white square for a centre, hoisted over a flag composed of three vertical bars coloured red white and blue, these flags representing P.T. in the International Code Pilotage Signal. In the night, a blue light every fifteen minutes, or a bright white light shown at intervals above the bulwarks.

Pin.—An iron bolt for the sheave of a block to travel on.

Pinch-gut.—A mean purser.

Pinch-gut pay.—Short allowance money.

Pinch-gut ship.—The name that used to be given to ships in which sailors were badly fed.

Pink.—A ship with a very narrow stern. The narrow stern rendered the quarter guns very serviceable.

Pink stern.—A high narrow stern.

Pinnace.—One of the boats of a man-of-war.

Pin-racks.—Hoops fitted with belaying-pins round a mast.

Pintles.—The pins on which a rudder works.

Pipe down!—The order to send such of the men below as are not wanted on deck

Piragua.—A canoe made out of the trunk of a tree. See *Robinson Crusoe*.

Pirate.—A robber on the high seas.

Pirate's flag.—Used to be a black field with a skull and battle-axe, sometimes an hour-glass.

Pisco.—A spirituous drink manufactured in Peru, and much drunk by sailors in the South Seas.

Pitch.—A thick black substance obtained by boiling down tar; also the action of a ship alternately heaving and depressing her bows; also the pitch of a screw propeller is the axial length of a whole turn of the thread.

Pitch-pole.—A sea is said to pitch-pole a boat when it hits her under the bows and throws her right up and down standing on her stern.

Pitch-poling.—A mode of killing whales by launching at them a lance to which is attached a warp to enable the harpooner to bring the lance back to his hand.

Pit-pan.—A flat-bottomed canoe.

Place.—The spot in which a ship is when at sea. Thus "everything relating to her place should be noted in the log;" that is, everything relating to the place she is in at the time of the occurrences.

Plane sailing.—An art of navigation based upon a supposition of the earth being an extended plane.

Plankage.—Charges on vessels in docks for the use of planks, for loading or unloading.

Plank it.—To plank it is to lie on the bare deck.

Planks.—Boards which cover the sides and form the decks of ships.

Plat.—Foxes braided.

Plate.—A sheet of iron or steel fixed to the frames of an iron vessel.

Plate-armour.—Steel or iron plates of great thickness on men-of-war, to render them shot-proof.

Plate-riders.—Diagonal iron plates fitted on the outside of the frames of fir-built ships of a certain tonnage and length.

Plate-ship.—The name given to the old galleons which were freighted with jewels, plate, and other treasure.

Platform.—A fabric used in smacks for keeping the ballast in its place.

Pledget.—The string of oakum used in caulking.

Plug,—A piece of metal, wood, or cork to fill the hole in the bottom of a boat. Also a piece of cake tobacco.

Plug-hole.—A hole in the bottom of a boat to let the water drain out as she hangs at the davits, or stands on the skids.

Plumb.—Straight up and down, as "to stay the fore-topmast plumb."

Plumber-blocks.—Blocks in a marine steam-ship in which the bushes are fixed in which the shafts or pinions revolve.

Plunger.—A small fast-sailing cutter with a centre board. Also a piston without valves.

Plunging fire.—Shot discharged from a higher level than that occupied by the object aimed at.

Ply.—To beat, to work to windward.

P.O.—Petty officer.

Pocket-bunker.—A bunker in the space between the cylinder of the engine and the sides of the boiler and upper stringers, and containing coal, usually the last used in a voyage.

Point.—To decorate a rope's end by working nettles over it.

Point-blank.—Aiming direct at the heart of the object without elevating the gun.

Polaccre.—A two-masted vessel, her lower and top masts in one, without tops: but with top-mast crosstrees and fidded topgallant masts.

Polar distance.—An arch of the meridian contained between the centre of an object and either pole of the equinoctial.

Pole.—A name given to the sky-sail masts. The end of a tall royal mast, from the yard when hoisted, to the truck is sometimes called the pole.

Pole-compass.—An inverted compass fixed on the top of a staff to remove it from local attraction.

Pole mast.—A **pole** mast is a single mast, such as some steamers are rigged with. Sky-sail **pole** is the name sometimes given to the sky-sail mast.

Poles.—Timbers for cargo consisting of the trunks of trees.

Pommelion.—The hindmost knob on the breech of a cannon.

Pontoon.—A portable boat used in fixing floating bridges.

Poop.—A raised after-deck.

Poop downhaul.—An imaginary rope, a seaman's jest, like "clapping the keel athwart-ships," and other such sayings.

Pooped.—Struck by a sea that washes over the stern.

Poop-house.—A house upon a raised quarter-deck for masters and mates, &c., to live in.

Poop-lantern.—A light shown by the flag-ship.

Poppets.—Timbers to support the bilgeways in launching.

Popple.—A sharp, cross sea, in water not very deep, as near a coast, in a bay, &c.

Port.—The left-hand side looking from the stern towards the bows.

Portage.—Tonnage.

Port bars.—Pieces of wood to secure the ports from flying open in bad weather.

Port-fire.—A signal that when ignited bursts forth into a shower of fire.

Port-flange.—A batten over a port to prevent water from washing in.

Port-hole.—A window for a cabin. An aperature in a ship's side to point a gun through.

Port-lids.—Covers for the ports in rough weather.

Port of registry.—The port at which a ship has been registered.

Portoise.—The gunwale.

Port pendants.—Ropes fixed to the outside of a port-lid for working it by a tackle.

Port-ropes.—For hauling up and suspending the ports.

Ports.—Large holes in the sides of a ship.

Port sashes.—Glazed half-ports or windows for the admission of light.

Port tack.—Sailing close to the wind blowing over the left-handbow.

Port the helm!—Shift the helm so as to force the vessel's head to the right.

Posted.—The old term for signifying the promotion from commander to captain.

Post-ship.—A name originally given to a twenty-gun ship to signify that she was of the lowest class to which a post-captain could be appointed.

Pouches.—Bulkheads for stowing purposes.

Pounders.—Said of a gun according to the weight of the ball it carries. Large guns are described by the diameter of their bore.

Powder-flag.—A red flag hoisted to indicate that the ship has gunpowder in her.

Powder-monkey.—Formerly a boy who had charge of the cartridge of the gun to which he belonged.

Pram.—A Norwegian lug-rigged slipper-shaped boat.

Pratique.—Licence to trade and have communication with a place after quarantine or on the production of a clean bill of health.

Prayer-book.—A small holystone.

Press-gang.—A number of men despatched from the crew of a man-of-war to seize merchant seamen and force them to serve in the navy.

Pressure.—Expansion or forcing power of steam calculated in pounds-weight upon the square inch of a boiler.

Preventer.—A rope used as an additional support for masts, booms, &c.

Preventer plates.—Additional irons for securing the chains.

Preventer stoppers.—Short ropes for securing the rigging in an engagement.

Preventive service.—The old name for the coastguard service.

Prick.—A mass of tobacco soaked in rum, and rolled up in canvas in a conical shape. Also a quantity of spun yarn laid up close.

Pricker.—A small marline-spike.

Pricking a chart.—Marking off on a chart the course made by a ship.

Pride of the morning.—A shower of rain.

Priming.—The boiling over of water in a boiler, due to muddy water. or to the commingling of different kinds of water, &c.

Prise.—To lift a weight with a handspike. To force anything open.

Prise-bolts.—Projections on a gun-carriage for the handspike to hold by, in raising the breech.

Prismatic compass.—A compass in which the divisions of the card are read by reflection at the same time that the bearing itself is taken.

Privateer.—A vessel furnished with a letter of marque.

Prize.—A vessel captured from an enemy.

Prize-officer.—An officer in charge of a ship captured from an enemy.

Prog.—Victuals.

Prong.—A small boat met with in Ireland. It has a high canoe-shaped stem, and is used by fishermen for boarding their vessels, or for ferrying, &c.

Protected men.—A term signifying merchant seamen not fit to serve in the Royal Navy.

Protractor.—A small semicircle of brass or horn, for drawing or measuring angles.

Provisional detention.—The detention of a ship by the Board of Trade for survey, either for her final detention or release.

Prow.—The poetical term for the stem or bows. Also the old name for a bumpkin.

Puddening.—Mats, yarns, oakum, &c., used as chafing gear.

Pulling.—Rowing.

Pump-barrel.—The tube in which the pump-rod or piston moves.

Pump-brake.—The handle of the primitive hand-pump.

Pumps.—There are many kinds of ship's pumps worked by steam or by a windmill or by hand.

Pump-spear.—The rod worked by the handle.

Pumps suck!—An exclamation to indicate that the vessel is free of the water that was to be pumped out.

Pump well.—An enclosure round the main-mast and pumps, where the water that penetrates a vessel collects.

Punt.—A little boat carried by small vessels.

Puoys.—Poles for driving barges or keels, by thrusting them laterally against the bottom of the river.

Purchase.—The power obtained by reeving a line through a block or blocks.

Purser.—Formerly a person on board a ship-of-war, who had charge of the provisions, clothes, &c.

Purser's dip.—A little dip candle.

Purser's grins.—"There are no half-laughs or purser's grins about me. I'm right up and down like a yard of pump water," meaning that the speaker is in earnest.

Purser's name.—A false name.

Purser's shirt.—"A purser's shirt on a handspike," said of ill-fitting clothes.

Putchers.—Contrivances used in the Bristol Channel for catching salmon. They are so fixed that the tide forces the fish into them.

Put off.—To quit a vessel, or the shore, in a boat.

Pyrites.—Gold-like scales in coal, and the cause of spontaneous combustion on board coal-freighted ships.

Q

Q.E.D.—The name of the first iron screw collier built in this country, 1844. She was an auxiliary.

Quadrant.—An instrument for measuring altitudes at sea. It consists of an *octant* or *frame*, an *arch* or *limb* and an *index*, and is furnished with a *nonius* or scale, index and horizon glasses, shades and sight vanes. Also a yoke.

Quadrant tiller.—A yoke shaped in the form of a quadrant. See yoke.

Quadrate.—To quadrate a gun is to adjust it on its carriage for level firing.

Quakers.—Sham guns, formerly used by merchantmen to frighten the enemy with an exhibition of strength.

Qualified pilot.—A person duly licensed by any pilotage authority to conduct a ship to which he does not belong.

Qualities.—A ship's capacity for sailing, carrying, and the like.

Quant.—A bargeman's long pole.

Quarantine.—The detention of a ship with sickness on board for a prescribed time, during which her people are allowed no intercourse with the shore.

Quarter.—The portion of a yard between the slings and the yard-arm. Also the after-sides of a ship. Also sparing the life of a conquered enemy. An old sea term. "The crew called for quarter."

Quarter-badge.—Ornamentation on the quarters of a ship.

Quarter-bill.—A list of the stations for men to take in time of action.

Quarter-blocks.—Blocks for the clew-lines and the sheets of the sail set above them to reeve through.

Quarter-boats.—Boats suspended on davits near the quarters.

Quarter-cask.—Half a hogshead.

Quarter-cloths.—Pieces of painted canvas over the quarter-netting.

Quarter-deck.—The after-deck of a flush-decked ship. When there is a poop, the quarter-deck extends from the break of the poop to a short distance forward.

Quarter-deckers.—The name given to officers who are sticklers for small points of etiquette, but who have little knowledge as seamen.

Quarter-fishes.—Stout pieces of wood hooped on to a mast to strengthen it.

Quarter-gallery.—A balcony that was formerly on the quarter of large ships.

Quarter-line.—Ships of a column ranged in a line, one being abaft another's beam.

Quarter-man.—A dockyard officer.

Quarter-master.—A person whose duty is to attend to the helm.

Quarter-nettings.—Nettings on the after-part of a ship for the stowage of hammocks.

Quarter-pieces.—Projections beyond the quarters of a ship for adding cabin accommodation there.

Quarter-ports.—Apertures in the after-sides.

Quarters.—The officers' and crew's stations in an engagement.

Quarter-slings.—Supports for a yard on either side the centre of it.

Quarter stops.—Fastenings to keep the bunt of a large sail snug in sending it up or down.

Quarter-tackle.—A tackle fitted to the quarter of the main-yard for hoisting or lowering heavy articles.

Quarter-watch.—An arrangement in men-of-war by which only one fourth of the crew have the watch on deck.

Quashee.—A West Indian negro.

Quicken.—To increase a curve.

Quick-work.—Short planks between the ports. All that part of a ship's side which lies between the chain wales and decks; so called because it was the work the quickest completed in building a ship.

Quid.—A piece of tobacco for chewing.

Quilting.—A coating for a vessel formed of ropes woven together. Also rope's-ending a man.

Quoin.—A wedge to support the breech of a gun for depressing or elevating it. Also a wedge to steady casks.

R

R.—An initial signifying "run," placed against the name of a deserter.

Rabbet.—The part of the stem and stem-post where the hood-ends fit into.

Race.—A strong tide. Also the engines of a steamer *race* when they work with great rapidity from the loss of resisting power, caused, for instance, by the breaking of the shaft or the dropping off of the propeller, or the raising of the stern of the ship, thereby lifting the screw out of the water.

Rack.—A fair-leader for running rigging.

Rack-bar.—A wooden lever.

Rack-block.—A piece of wood shaped into several blocks and used for fair-leaders.

Racking.—Seizing two ropes together.

Raddle.—To make flat work, such as boat's gripes, by interlacing.

Raffle.—Odds and ends of gear, a muddle of rigging such as might litter a deck from the fall of a mast, &c.

Raft-port.—A bow-port, sometimes a port under the counter for timber-loading.

Raft-dog.—A piece of flat iron with the ends bent.

Rafting.—To float timber or casks to or from a ship by binding them together.

Raise tacks and sheets!—An order in tacking to let go the fore and main tacks and main sheet.

Rake.—The inclination of a mast from the perpendicular. Also to sweep a ship's deck by firing along her whole length over her stem or bows.

Rakish.—Having the look of being fast and powerful.

Ram.—A projection at the stem of an iron-clad.

Ram-head.—A halliard-block.

Ram-line.—A line used for finding a straight middle line on a spar.

Ramming.—Driving a ship, furnished with a projection under her bows, stem on into another.

Ramshackle.—Disorderly. Said of a ship in a bad condition of hull and masts.

Randan fashion.—A boat rowed by a bow and stroke man, each pulling one oar, and a midship man pulling a pair of sculls.

Range.—Range alongside, to draw abreast. Also an extent of cable ranged along the deck ready for letting go the anchor.

Range-heads.—The windlass bitts.

Rap-full.—Said of a ship on a wind when her sails are clean full.

Rasing-iron.—A caulker's tool for cleaning seams.

Rate.—The rate of a chronometer is the difference of its daily errors. Also the *rating* of a seaman is his rank or position.

Rational horizon.—A circle parallel to the *sensible horizon* passing through the centre of the earth.

Ratlines.—Small ropes fastened to the shrouds, and forming a ladder.

Rat's tail.—A rope's end that tapers.

Rattle down.—To put on ratlines.

Rave-hook.—A tool for extracting oakum from seams.

Razee.—A line-of-battle ship cut down by one deck.

Ready about!—The order for all hands to go to their stations for tacking.

Rear-Admiral.—The admiral in command of the third division of a fleet. He carries his flag at the mizzen.

Rearing.—Said of the sides of a ship which are up and down like a wall.

Rear-ship.—The hindmost vessel of a fleet.

Rebojos.—Severe S.W. squalls encountered off the coast of Brazil.

Recall signals.—Lights or flags hoisted by a vessel to recall her boats.

Receiver of wreck.—A person appointed to take charge of any vessel stranded or in distress, and to receive depositions from mariners who have been in peril, &c.

Reckoning.—A ship's reckoning is the account of the vessel's position, by which it can be known at any time, approximately, where she is.

Red flag at masthead.—French privateers used to hoist this colour before an engagement, to signify that, if they conquered, they would give no quarter.

Reef.—To diminish the expanse of a sail by knotting the reef points in it upon the yard, or at the foot of a fore-and-aft sail.

Reef a bowsprit.—To reef a bowsprit is to heave it by a heel-rope in board to the required fid-hole, and then set up the gear again.

Reef-bands.—Bands of canvas across a sail to strengthen it for the reef-points.

Reef-becket.—A becket with a toggle for reefing. The end of the becket is passed under the reef-line and then toggled.

Reefer.—A midshipman.

Reefing paddles.—To reef a paddle-wheel is to disconnect the float-boards from the paddle-arms and secure them afresh nearer the centre of the wheel.

Reef in stays.—Reefing top-sails when in the act of tacking.

Reef knot.—A knot formed of two loops, one enclosing the other.

Reef-line.—A rope affixed across a sail for passing the beckets under in reefing.

Reef-pendant.—A rope in the after leech of a boom main-sail for bowsing down, with a tackle, the after-leech to the boom.

Reef-tackles.—Tackles to haul out the leech of a sail to the yard-arms when reefing it.

Reef-tackle spans.—Cringles in the bolt-rope.

Reeming.—Opening seams for the admission of caulking.

Reeming-beetle.—A large mallet.

Reeming-iron.—The tool used in opening the seams.

Reeve.—To pass a rope through a block or any aperture or eye.

Refit.—To repair damages. To put the rigging into proper condition.

Refraction.—The difference between the real and apparent place of a heavenly body.

Register.—A ship's register is a document giving her name, tonnage, official number, &c.

Registrar-General of Seamen.—An officer appointed to keep a register of all persons who serve in ships which come under the provisions of the Merchant Shipping Acts.

Relieve.—To relieve is to replace a man by another, so that he may rest. "Relieve the wheel," an order for a man to take the helmsman's place at the end of two hours.

Relieving tackles.—Tackles hooked on the tiller to help the helm in heavy weather.

Render.—To pass a rope through a place. A rope is also said to render when it surges or slips. Also to yield. A cable is rendered when it is eased.

Respondentia.—Money lent on security of cargo.

Retard.—A term applied to the time that has elapsed between the moon's transit, at which a tide originated, and the appearance of the tide itself.

Revenue-cutter.—An armed, single-masted vessel for preventing smuggling.

Reverse valve.—A valve fixed on or near the top of a marine boiler, to prevent the straining of the boiler by the outside atmosphere when a vacuum takes place in the boiler.

Rhumb-line.—A track on the earth's surface that cuts all the meridians at the same angle. Also rhumb-lines are the lines which divide the compass card into thirty-two points.

Ribbands.—Pieces of timber nailed outside the ribs of a wooden ship.

Ribbing-nail.—A large nail used in wooden ship building.

Rickers.—Poles used in stowing flax, &c.

Ride.—To ride at anchor, to lie at anchor. "She rode easily," said of a ship making good weather when hove-to in a storm.

Ride down.—To hang on to halliards, so as to help with one's weight the men who are hauling. Also to come down a stay for tarring it.

Riders.—Timber from the keelson to the orlop beams for additional strength. Also casks stowed above the ground tier. Also contrivances for strengthening a wooden ship against hogging and sagging strains.

Ridge-ropes.—The ropes to which an awning is stretched. Also life-lines, stretched along in foul weather.

Riding-bitts.—The bitts to which a cable is fastened when a ship is at anchor.

Riding-light.—A lantern hoisted or shown on board a vessel at anchor.

Rig.—The rig of a vessel means her character; as brig-rig, barque-rig, ship-rig, &c. Also to fit all the rigging to a ship's masts.

Rig in.—To draw a boom in.

Rig out.—To run a boom out. Also to dress or outfit a person.

Rig the capstan.—To ship the bars ready for heaving.

Rigger.—A man whose vocation is that of rigging vessels.

Rigging.—Standing rigging consists of all those ropes which are fixed, such as shrouds, backstays, &c. Running rigging of all those ropes which can be pulled upon, such as halliards, clew-lines, &c.

Rigging-mats.—Chafing-mats.

Right ascension.—The right ascension of a celestial body is an arch of the equinoctial contained between the first point of Aries and the point of the equinoctial cut by a meridian passing through the object.

Right-handed.—A rope the strands of which are laid with the sun, i.e. from right to left.

Righting.—Said of a ship that recovers herself after having been thrown on her beam-ends.

Right the helm.—Put it amidships; in a line with the keel.

Right up and down.—Said of a dead calm.

Rim.—The edge of a top.

Ring.—An iron hoop at the upper extremity of the shank of an anchor for attaching the cable to.

Ring-bolt.—A ring fitted to an eye-bolt.

Ring-stopper.—Rope secured to a ring-bolt and attached to the cable through other ring-bolts as a precaution in veering.

Ring-tail.—A small sail, shaped like a jib and set outside the spanker.

Rivet.—A bar of metal used for securing the plates of an iron ship to the frames.

Roach.—The curve in the foot of a sail.

Road.—An anchorage clear of the shore.

Roband.—A piece of line or sennit at the head of a sail to attach it to the jackstay.

Roband hitch.—A hitch for securing the pieces of rope which secure a sail to the jackstay.

Rocket.—A signal of distress. Also a means of firing a line to a ship in distress.

Rocket-apparatus.—A contrivance for throwing a line to a ship by a rocket; a block and rove line are then conveyed, by means of which a hawser is sent aboard, and the men are brought ashore in a cradle or breeches buoy.

Rode of all.—An order to throw in the oars of a boat.

Roger.—One of the names of the pirate's flag.

Rogue's yarn.—A yarn in a rope for detecting its theft.

Roll.—To sway from side to side in contradistinction to pitch.

Rollers.—A violent swell during a calm; attributed to the earthquake wave, but the origin is not satisfactorily known.

Rolling hitch.—A hitch for attaching the tail of a jigger, &c., to a rope.

Rolling tackles.—Tackles for steadying the yards in rough weather.

Rombowline.—Old rope, canvas, &c.

Rooming.—Running to leeward.

Rope.—A line composed of threads of hemp, coir, manilla, steel, or other stuff. The threads are called yarns; the yarns are twisted into strands, and the strands laid up into rope. Also to rope a sail is to affix ropes, called the bolt-ropes, to the sides of it all round, in order to strengthen it, &c.

Rope funnel.—A funnel formerly used, when a better was not to be had, for filling water-casks, and was made by flemishing a length of rope down, stopping the parts at each turn with rope yarns, and then turning it inside out so as to form a cone.

Ropemaker's eye.—An eye or loop in a hemp cable formed by two strands twisted up on the bight.

Ropes.—"To know the ropes"—to know his business.

Rope's-ending.—Beating a man or boy with the end of a rope.

Rope yarn.—A thread of any stuff of which ropes are made.

Ropeyarn knot.—A knot used in tying yarns together, formed by splitting the ends of two yarns, and knotting one of the split parts.

Rose.—A strainer at the heel of a pump to prevent choking.

Rose-lashing.—Lashing used for the eyes of rigging, &c.

Roster.—A list for routine on any particular duty.

Rough-tree.—An unfinished mast or spar.

Round charter.—A charter on a round of voyages.

Round dozen.—Thirteen lashes when men were flogged.

Round-house.—A cabin built on deck roofed by the poop.

Round in.—To haul, as "round in the weather braces."

Rounding.—A sort of small junk, unlaid. Also rope round a large rope.

Round shot.—A single solid iron shot of various weights.

Round up.—To haul upon a tackle.

Rouse.—To haul taut; to pull in or drag forward.

Roving commission.—Liberty to an officer in command of a ship of war to cruise wherever he thinks proper.

Rowle.—A small crane.

Rowlocks.—Brass forks in a boat's gunwale for rowing. Also holes cut in the gunwale for the oars.

Row-ports.—Apertures in the sides of a vessel near the water for sweeps.

Royal.—A light sail set over the topgallant-sail.

Royal masthead.—The upper end of the topmost mast of a ship, unless skysail masts are carried.

Royal yard.—The yard above the topgallant yard to which the royal is bent.

Rubber.—A contrivance for flattening the seams of a sail in sail-making.

Rudder-bands.—The hinges of the rudder. Also called braces.

Rudder chains.—Affixed to the hinder part of the rudder and worked by tackle when the tiller is damaged.

Rudder-rake.—The hinder part of the rudder.

Rudder-rods.—Rods fitting over sheaves, and used to steer steamers from the bridge.

Rudder-trunk.—A casing of wood fitted into the helm port for the rudder-stock to work in.

Rule of the Road.—Regulations for controlling the navigation of vessels in rivers and seas, for the avoidance of collisions, &c.

Rumbo.—Stolen rope.

Rum-gagger.—A sham sailor who begs.

Run.—The hollow curving in a vessel's bottom that rises and narrows under the quarters.

Rundle.—The upper part of a capstan.

Rungheads.—Floor timber ends.

Run goods.—Goods which have been smuggled ashore.

Rungs.—Floor timbers.

Runlet.—A measure of eighteen gallons and a half.

Run money.—The money paid to the crew of a coaster for a short trip. Also money paid for apprehending a deserter.

Runner.—A crimp, one who furnishes crews. Also the cant name for a crimp. Also a single rope rove through a movable block. And formerly, a vessel that sailed without a convoy in time of war.

Runner and tackle.—A single block fitted with a lashing; the runner is rove through it and spliced round the double block of a tackle, of which the single block is fitted with a hook.

Running.—Sailing with the wind over the stern.

Running agreement.—An agreement entered into by a crew to make two or more voyages in a foreign-going ship, whose voyages average less than six months in duration.

Running bowline.—A bowline with the standing part running through it, forming a noose.

Running bowsprit.—A bowsprit, such as a cutter's, that can be slided in and out.

Running rigging.—All the ropes of a ship which lead through blocks, &c., and can be hauled and worked. Also called running gear.

Ryak.—An Esquimaux boat, built of wood, whalebone, &c. and covered with skins. It has a round hole in the centre, in which the occupant sits.

S

Saddle.—A piece of wood fitted to a yard, hollowed for the upper part of a boom to rest in.

Saddle of jib boom.—A piece of wood affixed to the bowsprit to steady the heel of the jib boom.

Saddle of spanker boom.—A support for the jaws of the spanker boom on the mizzen-trysail mast.

Safety-valve.—A valve affixed to the marine boiler, and so arranged that when the steam in the boiler gets to any given pressure, the valve lifts and allows the steam to escape.

Sag.—To drift bodily.

Sagged.—A ship is said to be *sagged* when her bottom curves downwards through straining.

Sail-burton.—See Sail-tackle.

Sail-hook.—A hook for holding the seams of a sail whilst sewing it.

Sailing-gig.—An open boat fitted with a battened lug-sail.

Sailor's blessing.—A curse.

Sailor's pleasure.—Yarning, smoking, dancing, growling, &c.

Sailor's waiter.—A term applied to the second mate of small vessels.

Sails are square or fore-and-aft. A square sail is fastened to a yard and hoisted up a mast. A fore-and-aft sail is fastened to a gaff or travels on a stay, or sets "flying," that is, hoisted taut on its own luff.

"Sails."—The sailor's name for a ship's carpenter.

Sail signals.—A method of signalling by means of setting or furling topgallant sails and royals.

Sail-tackle.—A tackle hooked round the topmast head, used in sending a top-sail aloft for bending.

Saker.—An old piece of ordnance used in ships. It is supposed to have thrown a six-pound shot.

Salinometer.—An instrument for showing the saline density of water in marine engines.

Sally-port.—A large opening on each quarter of a fire-ship through which the people who fired the train escaped. Also the port by which a three-decker was entered.

Salt.—A sailor.

Salvage.—The saving of a vessel or any portion of her cargo from a situation of peril or after shipwreck.

Salvage bond.—A bond signed by the master, binding the owners of the ship and cargo to pay a given sum, to be afterwards proportioned by the High Court of Admiralty, to the persons who have rendered the salvage services admitted to have been performed in the bond.

Salvo.—A discharge of several guns all together.

Sampan.—A small Chinese boat.

Sampson-post.—A timber structure fitted with a bell to sound in a fog.

Sand-glass.—A glass containing sand that runs for fourteen or twenty-eight seconds, used in heaving the log.

Sand-strake.—A name for the garboard strake.

Saucer.—An iron socket in which the foot of a capstan revolves.

Save-all.—A sail under a lower studding-sail to catch the wind under the boom.

Sawed off square.—Said of a ship with an up-and-down stem and stern.

Scalding down.—Blowing hot water over a marine engine for cleansing it.

Scale.—Crust that collects upon the inside of a marine boiler.

Scale pan.—A large shallow pan for receiving the insoluble particles of salt or "scale" from marine boilers.

Scaling hammers.—Hammers for removing the scale.

Scandalizing.—Hauling up the tack of a fore-and-aft sail and lowering the peak.

Scantling.—The strength or thickness of iron or wooden sides. Literally, the sides themselves.

Scarph.—The connexion of one piece of timber with the other by the overlapping of the ends.

Schooner.—A two-masted vessel rigged with fore-and-aft sails. A topsail schooner has square yards forward. A two-topsail schooner has square yards on both masts. A three-masted schooner has three masts, all rigged with fore-and-aft canvas.

Schuyt.—A Dutch vessel rigged like a galliot.

Scoffing.—Eating. To *scoff* a thing is to eat it.

Scope.—Length, as a long scope of cable.

Score.—The groove cut in the side and bottom of a block to fit the strop to.

Scotch coffee.—Hot water flavoured with burnt biscuit.

Scotchman.—A piece of wood fitted to a shroud or any other standing rope to save it from being chafed.

Scotch-prize.—A capture by mistake.

Scow.—A kind of lighter.

Scowbank.—One of the crew of a scow. A term of contempt addressed to a sailor.

Scraper.—A triangular iron instrument for scraping the deck. Also a cocked hat.

Screw-alley.—Also called the tunnel. An avenue direct from the engine-room of a steamer leading as far aft as the stern-tube bulkhead.

Screw-well.—An aperture over the screw of an auxiliary for allowing the propeller to be lifted.

Scribe.—To mark packages in bond with the number and weight.

Scrimp.—Small, faint, as "a scrimp wind."

Scrimshandy.—An Americanism signifying the objects in ivory or bone carved by whalemen during their long voyages.

Scrive board.—A number of planks clamped edge to edge together, and painted black. On these boards are marked with a sharp tool the lines of the sections or frames which have been previously drawn upon it. Used in iron ship-building.

Scrowl.—A piece of timber fixed to the knees of the head.

Scud.—To drive before a gale.

Scudders.—The name given to fishermen, who, in hauling in the nets, shake the meshes in order to jerk out the fish.

Scuffle-hunters.—Formerly a set of men who offered their services on board a discharging ship; they wore long aprons, in which to hide whatever they could steal.

Scull.—A small oar. Also to propel a boat by working an oar over the stern.

Scupper-leather.—A flap of leather outside a scupper hole, to prevent water from entering.

Scupper-ports.—Apertures in an iron steamer's bulwarks for freeing the decks from water.

Scuppers.—The gutter of a ship's decks, the water-ways.

Scuttle.—To sink a ship by boring holes in her. Also the fore-scuttle (which see).

Scuttle-butt.—A cask on deck in which fresh water is kept.

Scuttles.—Small holes in the ship's sides for lighting and ventilating.

Sea-anchor.—Spars lashed together and flung overboard, to prevent a ship hove-to from falling into the trough of the sea.

Sea-board.—Where land and water meet.

Sea-boots.—Tall boots well greased, used in washing down in cold weather, &c.

Sea-cunny.—A term that often occurs in the old marine annals. It means a Lascar quarter-master.

Sea-day.—A day that begins at noon and ends on the following noon. It begins twelve hours earlier than the civil day.

Sea gear.—Running rigging that is used in setting and taking in sail, &c., at sea, but which is unrove in harbour for neatness and to preserve it.

Sea-going.—Fit for the sea. As "in sea-going trim."

Sea-lawyers.—Scheming sailors, versed in marine law, so far at least as it concerns the forecastle, and capable, like Midshipman Easy, of arguing the point with captains.

Sea-legs.—The capacity of walking the decks of a rolling ship without staggering.

Sea-licence.—A special licence qualifying the person to whom it is granted to act as pilot for any part of the sea beyond the limits of any pilotage authority.

Seams.—The joints of the external planking. Also the places where the cloths are sewn together in a sail.

Sea-work.—The account of the ship's way, &c., entered in the log at sea.

Sea-worthiness.—Tight, staunch, strong, and in every way fitted for the voyage.

Second hand.—The man next to the one in charge of a smack.

Second mate.—An officer in the merchant service. He ranks after the first or chief mate, and heads the starboard watch.

Second rate.—A ship of seventy-four guns was so called.

Secret block.—A sheave in a shell with holes in one extremity, large enough to receive the rope.

"See all clear for stays!"—An order preparatory to tacking a ship.

Seizing.—The laniard, line, or stuff, with which anything is made fast. To seize, is to make a thing fast, by securing it to a place; as to seize a flag in the rigging.

Selvagee.—Rope-yarns worked into a bight and marled with spun-yarn. Used as block-strops, &c.

Semaphore.—A signal consisting of arms, whose different postures signify certain meanings.

Send down.—To send down a yard, is to cast off all the rigging, bend the yard-rope to the slings, and stop it to the quarters; sway away, to remove the lifts and braces, and then lower. A mast is sent down by a mast rope.

Send or Scend.—The impulse of a wave by which a ship is carried bodily.

Senior officer.—The officer in command of a ship or squadron for the time being.

Sennit.—Rope-yarns twisted into foxes and plaited.

Sensible horizon.—The line described by sea and water where they meet.

Serang.—An Asiatic boatswain.

Serons.—Bullocks' hides in which South American indigo is packed.

Serve.—To supply a gun with ammunition and to handle it.

Service.—Small stuff laid tightly round a rope.

Serving-board.—A wooden implement for laying small stuff upon a rope.

Serving-mallet.—A wooden implement used for laying spun-yarn or other small stuff on a large rope.

Serving out.—Giving the allowance of provisions, water, or rum, to the crew.

Set.—The set of a current is the compass direction it moves in.

Set flying.—Said of sails which are set from the deck or tops, such as a studding-sail.

Setting.—To pole a boat or barge along.

Setting-up.—To set up rigging is to bring it taut.

Settle.—To sink slowly; to founder. A whale *settles* when it sinks bodily in a horizontal position without moving tail or fin. Also to lower slowly, as "Settle away those halliards!"

Sextant.—An instrument with an arch of 120° for measuring angular distances to determine the longitude. It is constructed on the same principle as a quadrant, but is furnished with more appliances than that instrument, to insure greater accuracy.

Shackle iron.—An iron bar for drawing bolts.

Shade errors.—Errors due to inequality of the glass of the coloured shades of a sextant.

Shafting.—The connected shafts or lengths of steel or iron bars to which the propeller of a screw-steamer is attached.

Shaft stool.—The base of the shaft bearings in the tunnel of a screw-steamer.

Shake-out.—To unknot the reef-points in order to expand more of the sail.

Shaking.—Shaking a cask is knocking it into staves which are made into bundles.

Shakings.—Old canvas, rope, &c.

Shallop.—A boat formerly carried by ships.

Shallow-waisted.—Said of a flush-decked ship where there is no poop nor top-gallant forecastle to make a well.

Shank.—The middle piece of an anchor.

Shank-painter.—The rope or chain by which an anchor is secured to a ship's side.

Shanty.—A small house. Sailor's name for a bad house.

Shaping course.—"We *shaped our course* for such-and-such a port," meaning. "We headed the ship for the port in question, and steered for it."

Shark's-mouth.—That part of an awning that fits round a mast.

Sharp up.—When the yards are braced hard against the lee rigging.

Shear-legs.—Appliances used for getting out and landing heavy weights, such as boilers, machinery, engines, &c., also for masting and dismasting vessels.

Shear-pole.—A pole for swifting in the rigging to put the ratlines on.

Shears.—Spars lashed together at angles, and used for taking in masts.

Sheathing.—The metal on a ship's bottom, usually called yellow metal.

Sheathing-boards.—Boards formerly affixed to the bottom of vessels to protect them from sea-worms, &c.

Sheath-knife.—A knife carried in a sheath fitted to a belt round the waist.

Sheave.—The wheel inside a block which revolves with the rope that is hauled through it.

Shebeen.—A low public-house.

Sheepshank.—Half hitches over the ends of the bight in a rope, to shorten it without cutting.

Sheer.—The curve of a ship's deck towards the head and stern. Also called spring.

Sheer-batten.—A piece of wood fixed to the shrouds above the dead-eyes to prevent them from turning.

Sheer-drawing.—A drawing of a ship composed of three parts, i.e. the sheer plan, the half-breadth plan, and the body plan.

Sheer hulk.—An old dismasted, useless hull.

Sheering.—The shaping of any ship upwards.

Sheer off.—To shift the helm and get away.

Sheer-plan.—A drawing descriptive of half of the longest and widest and level section in a ship.

Sheer-streak.—The first plank below the covering-board.

Sheet-bend.—A bend for joining two ropes.

Sheet home.—An order to haul by means of the sheets the outer corners or clews of the sails to the yard-arms.

Sheets.—Ropes attached to the lower corners of square sails, and the after lower corners of fore-and-aft sails.

Sheeve ho!—A cry raised when the blocks of a tackle come together.

Shelf.—Internal ribs of wood along the whole length of a vessel to receive the ends of the beams.

Shell.—The outside portion of the case of a boiler. Also a projectile filled with a bursting charge. Also the outside part of a block.

Shelter-deck.—A name given to a deck that extends throughout a ship's length and breadth. Such terms are quite new and apparently arbitrary, and consequently any attempt to define them must be unsatisfactory.

Shift.—To shift a sail is to unbend it and replace it by another.

Shifting-boards.—Movable boards in the hold of a ship to prevent the cargo from shifting in a sea-way.

Shimal.—A gale encountered in the Persian Gulf.

Shingle-tramper.—A coast-guardsman.

Ship.—A three-masted vessel with square yards, tops and top-mast crosstrees on each mast. Also, in law, any kind of vessel used in navigation, not propelled by oars.

Ship-boy.—An apprentice. A cabin boy. The term is obsolete.

Ship-chandler.—A tradesman who supplies ships with marine stores.

Ship-keeper.—A person who has charge of a ship in harbour when there is no crew aboard.

Shipmate.—Sailor's word for brother-worker. One of a crew having relation to that crew. Messmate is one of a watch, having relation to that watch, because the members of it take their meals together.

Shipper.—One who embarks goods.

Shipping-bills.— Papers containing particulars of the cargo to be shipped.

Shipping-master.—A person appointed to superintend the engagement and discharge of seamen, and to perform other duties.

Shipping-office.—An office where crews are engaged by captains, and where they sign articles.

Ship's cousin.—One who lives aft, yet has to do the work of a foremast hand.

Ship's husband.—A person to whom the management of a ship is entrusted by or on behalf of the owner.

Ship-shape and Bristol fashion.—Spick and span. Everything smart above and below.

Ship-sloop.—Formerly a twenty-four-gun vessel that was rated as a ship when commanded by a captain.

Shipwright surveyor.—A person appointed to report upon the construction, life-saving equipment, water-tight bulkheads, &c., of iron and wooden ships.

Shiver.—To shiver a sail is to shake the wind out of it by luffing or bracing the yards to the wind.

Shoot the sun.—Taking its altitude.

Shop.—A dock term applied to three or more packages of tea arranged for the inspection of the brokers.

Shore.—To prop up a ship or anything with spars called shores.

Shore-anchor.—The anchor, when a ship is moored, that is between the shore and the ship.

Shore-cleats.—Pieces of wood fixed on a vessel's side to support the shore-head when the ship is shored upright.

Shore-fast.—A rope that secures the vessel to anything on shore.

Short allowance.—A reduction in the quantity of provisions or water served out.

Short-handed.—Said of a ship without enough hands to work her properly.

Short-linked chain.—A chain without studs and consequently short-linked.

Short sea.—A quick jerky sea.

Short service.—Formerly said of chafing gear in a short range of hemp cable.

Short sheet.—A rope attached to the inner corner of a topmast studding-sail and belayed in the top.

Short splice.—A connexion formed by passing the six strands of two ropes over and under one another, and dividing the yarns so as to taper the splice.

Short topgallant mast.—A topgallant mast fitted with crosstrees above which a royal mast may be rigged and secured by a fid. See Stump topgallant mast.

Shot in the locker.—Money possessed by a seaman. "There is still a shot left in the locker," or "the locker is low."

Shot-lockers.—Places where the shot is kept in men-of-war, usually on each side of the fire-magazine.

Shot racks.—Iron rods fitted to hold shot.

Shot soup.—A name given to the pea-soup served out to the forecastle on account of the bullet-like hardness of the peas in it.

Shoulder-block.—A block with a projection in the shell to prevent the rope from jamming against the spar to which the block is affixed.

Shout.—A kind of punt used for shooting wild fowl. Also, standing drinks all round.

Shovel.—A term of contempt applied to an incapable marine engineer.

Show a leg!—"Show a leg, there!" means, "Show yourself" on the order being given to turn out.

Shrapnel.—Projectiles of shell for long range filled with bursting charge and bullets.

Shroud-laid.—A rope whose strands are laid from right to left.

Shrouds.—Ropes for the support of masts. They were formerly hemp, but are now nearly always of wire.

Shroud trucks.—Pieces of perforated wood seized to the standing rigging as fair-leaders for the running rigging.

Shrub.—An intoxicating drink sold in Calcutta to seamen.

Shuffle-board.—A game of quoits played on board ship.

Sick flag.—A name for the quarantine flag.

Sick mess.—The mess into which the sick men of a man-of-war's crew are put.

Side ladder.—The gangway ladder (which see).

Side-men.—Men who attend the gangway to hand the side-ropes, &c., when a boat containing an officer or anybody of importance comes alongside.

Side or sister keelsons.—Timbers inside the frame of a ship abreast of the main-mast to strengthen the vessel in that part.

Side-pieces.—The name given to certain parts of a made mast.

Sidereal day.—The interval between the transit of a star over a meridian and its return to the same meridian.

Side-rods.—These are rods on each side the cylinder of a marine engine for producing a simultaneous movement.

Side-steps.—Small pieces of wood fixed to the side of a ship to serve as steps for climbing aboard.

Side-valve casing.—A cover to the nozzles or steam-ports on one side of the cylinder of a marine engine.

Sights.—Taking sights—taking an observation. *To sight a mast* is to watch it whilst it is being stayed.

Sight the anchor.—This is to heave it up until it shows, that it may be seen clear.

Signal-man.—A first-class petty officer in the navy who has charge of the signals.

Signal-stations.—Stations on the coast of England and abroad with which ships can communicate by means of the International Code of Signals.

Sill.—A piece of timber against which the gates of a dock close.

Silt.—Mud or shingle thrown up by the action of the tide.

Single.—To single a purchase is to unreeve the running part of it.

Single boating system.—Smacks fishing singly instead of in fleets. See Fleeting.

Single top-sail.—A whole top-sail—that is, the sail not divided by a yard. See Double top-sails.

Single-whip.—A single rope rove through a fixed block.

Sing out!—To call, to hail. "Sing Out!" also means, "Shout louder!"

Sing song.—Sailor's name for a Chinese theatre.

Sinnit.—Grass laid lip in plaits and used by sailors for making hats. See Sennit.

Siren.—A horn for sounding blasts in foggy weather.

Sir-mark.—A particular mark to guide workmen in ship-building.

Sister-block.—Two blocks formed out of one piece of wood.

Six upon four.—Said of six men put upon rations which would be the usual allowance of four men.

Six-water grog.—Rum diluted by six times its quantity of water; reckoned a poor drink by Jack in old days, though in this age he gets nothing stronger than limejuice.

Skeel.—The name of a large kid or tub.

Skeet.—A scoop that was formerly used for wetting sails in light winds to accelerate the pace of the ship.

Skid-beams.—Supports on which booms and boom-boats are stowed.

Skids.—Large fenders over a ship's side. Also supports on which boats are stowed on deck.

Skiff.—A long slender boat with a hole in the centre fitted with a sliding seat, used in rowing matches. It has nothing to do with sailors.

Skin.—To skin a sail is to roll it up taut and smoothly in the headband. Also the interior sides of a ship's hold.

Skulls.—Small oars.

Sky-larking.—Horse-play; acting the fool.

Sky-light.—A glazed frame over a cabin, engine-room, &c., for the admission of light and air.

Sky-sail.—A small square sail that sets on a pole above the royal-mast.

Sky-sail-pole.—A mast on which the sky-sail yard travels. It is a continuation of the royal mast.

Sky-scraper.—An imaginary sail set along with moon-sails, angel's foot-stools, and the like, jokingly assumed to be carried by Yankees.

Slab.—The slack part of a sail.

Slab-line.—A rope to haul up the foot or slab of a course.

Slack helm.—Said of a ship that carries a lee helm.

Slack in stays.—Slow in tacking; slow when in the act of going about.

Slack water.—The state of water in the pause between the flux and reflux of the tide.

Slatting.—The violent shaking of a fore-and-aft sail when in the wind or when being hauled down.

Sleepers.—Two cross-pieces over the top. Also knees which connect the transoms with the after timbers on a ship's quarter.

Sleep in.—To remain in bed without being roused up to come on deck. To sleep through your watch on deck or all night.

Slew.—To turn.

Slewed.—Intoxicated.

Slice.—An instrument used for clearing the air-spaces between the bars of a furnace.

Slide-valve.—A valve that works on a cylinder-face for admitting steam to the upper and lower ports of the cylinder alternately.

Sliding gunters.—Masts fitted abaft a mast, and which may be easily got up and taken down.

Sliding keel.—A keel that may be lowered or raised at will by a winch or other apparatus.

Sling.—Passing a rope round anything to hoist it.

Sling-band.—A stout iron band round the centre of a lower yard with an eyebolt on top to which the slings are attached.

Sling-dogs.—Two iron implements shackled together and used in lifting timber.

Slings.—A chain or rope that suspends the centre of a yard. Hence "in the slings" means in the bunt or middle of a yard.

Slip.—The loss of propelling power in the revolution of paddle wheels or a screw, due to the yielding of water; also to let a cable go overboard, to save the time that would be occupied in heaving up the anchor.

Slip-hooks.—Patent hooks for holding a boat at the davits; when the boat is lowered the hooks fly open and release her.

Slippery hitch.—A hitch or knot that *gives* when a strain is put upon it.

Slip-rope.—A rope bent to the cable and brought to the weather quarter.

Slip-shackle.—A shackle with a lever for letting go suddenly.

Slip-stopper.—A chain for stoppering the cable, for clearing hawse, unbitting, &c.

Slipway.—An inclined plane from which ships are launched.

Slives.—Heavy spars used in stowing hides.

Slobgollion.—Whaleman's term for an oozy, stringy substance found in sperm oil.

Sloop.—A one-masted vessel with a standing bowsprit and fore-sail that sets on a stay.

Sloop-of-war.—A brig or corvette ship. She sometimes mounted eighteen guns, and, if deep waisted, twenty-six or twenty-eight.

Slops.—Clothes kept on board to sell to the crew.

Slop-shop.—A ready-made clothing shop for seamen usually kept by crimps.

Sludge.—Thin spongy ice formed upon the surface of the ocean.

Slush.—Grease from the galley coppers used for greasing down the masts and making puddings for sailors.

Slush-bucket.—A bucket for holding grease, taken aloft for "greasing down."

Slush-lamp.—A lamp used in some ships' forecastle; it is fed by the filthy matter skimmed off the surface of the cook's coppers. It is monstrous that owners' parsimony should force sailors to use this vile-smelling light.

Smack.—A fishing-vessel, sometimes dandy-rigged, sometimes cutter-rigged with a jib that sets flying.

Smacksmooth.—Flush, as when a mast breaks short off the deck.

Small-arms-men.—The portion of a man-of-war's crew trained to the use of muskets, pistols, cutlasses and other weapons which are called small arms.

Small stuff.—See Stuff.

Smart-money.—The pension given to wounded men.

Smasher.—A north-country seaman. Also the name by which the carronade used to be called.

Smiting-line.—A line used to loose a sail when confined by rope-yarns.

Smoke-box.—A large receptacle for smoke in a steamer. The foot of the funnel is fitted into it through the funnel casing.

Smoke-sail.—A piece of canvas extended before the galley chimney to prevent the smoke from blowing aft when the vessel is head to wind.

Snags.—Stumps of trees which impede river navigation.

Snaking.—Winding small rope round backstays and stays and other large ropes, used in an engagement as a preventer should the rigging be severed. Also to pass small stuff round a seizing with marling hitches at the outer turns.

Snatch-block.—A block into which a rope can be slipped without passing the end through the sheave-hole. The iron strop has a hinge to enable it to be lifted and closed.

Sneer.—To strain a vessel by carrying a heavy press of canvas.

Sneezer.—A gale of wind.

Snifting valve.—A valve in a marine steam-engine connected with the condenser by a pipe under the air-pump. When pressed by steam entering the condenser it opens, otherwise it is kept shut by the pressure of the atmosphere.

Snotter.—A rope loop to prevent slipping, as, for instance, a block which is kept in its place at a boom-end by this loop. Also a rope for bending a tripping line to in sending down royal and topgallant yards.

Snow.—A vessel rigged like a brig, the only difference being that she has a try-sail mast for her try-sail.

Snub.—To bring up suddenly with an anchor and short range of cable. Also to check a rope suddenly.

Snug.—A ship is said to be snug when she is prepared to meet bad weather.

Sny.—An upward bend in a piece of timber.

So!—An exclamation to signify, "That will do!" "Enough!" "No higher," &c.

Socket signal.—A rocket discharged from a socket to a great height, where it explodes with much noise. It is fired by a friction tube attached to a lanyard.

Soft-tack.—Bread as distinct from biscuit, which is called ship's bread.

Soger.—A soldier. A term of contempt applied to a sailor.

Sogering.—Loafing, skulking, idling, making pretend to work.

Solar day.—The interval between the sun's departure from and return to the same meridian.

Soldier's wind.—A fair wind either way, outwards or homewards; therefore a beam wind or thereabouts.

Sole piece.—A piece of timber on the heel of the rudder, meant to come easily off, should the ship take the ground.

Sole plate.—A plate that forms the foundation for a marine engine to rest on.

Solid bottomed.—Said of a vessel with close timbers in her bottom, no limbers and no proper water-ways. Any water, therefore, that a ship so built makes, has to find its way to the pump well through the ballast.

Solstitial points.—Two points of the ecliptic 90° distant from the equinoctial points.

Soniwax, or Sonnywax.—A term used by sailors when addressing boys. "Look here, my soniwax, turn to and," &c. It is probably meant as a marine diminutive of son.

Sound.—To heave the lead. To plumb the bottom. A whale sounds when it throws its flukes aloft and sinks head foremost.

Sounding machine.—A machine dropped overboard and operated on by the water that turns a fan whose motion is communicated to the register wheels by which the depth of the water is shown.

Sounding-rod.—A rod marked with a scale of feet and inches, for dropping into the well to ascertain the depth of water.

Soundings.—In soundings, is being in water whose bottom can be reached by the lead. Soundings is the name given to the entrance of the English Channel between latitude 48° and 49°.

Soup and bouilli.—Pronounced soup and bully, and nicknamed by Jack, soap and bullion: preserved meat, vegetables, &c., in soup—usually horribly nauseous.

Southerly-buster.—A sudden gale from the southward in Australian latitudes.

Southing.—Distance made good to the south.

Sou'-wester.—A waterproof covering for the head, with a thatch down the back for the water to drain off by.

Space system.—A mode of ventilating a ship's hold freighted with bags of rice. A tunnel is formed of the bags, placed fore and aft, leaving an empty space about a foot wide which forms the ventilating tunnel. This is also known as Heap's system.

Span.—A rope made fast at both ends for hooking a block to the bight of it.

Span-blocks.—Blocks at the head of the top-mast and topgallant-mast for studding-sail halliards to reeve through.

Span-irons.—Harpoons secured to the sides of a whale-boat above the thwarts.

Spanish burton.—A tackle consisting of two single blocks, one fixed, the other movable.

Spanish foxes.—Single rope-yarns unlaid and then rolled up. See Foxes.

Spanish reef.—The yards on the cap.

Spanish windlass.—A purchase for bringing two taut ropes together.

Spanker.—The fore-and-aft gaff-sail on the mizzen-mast of a ship or barque. Also called mizzen and driver.

Spanking.—Sailing swiftly along with the wind so quartered as to keep the spanker full.

Spanner.—A key for screwing up nuts.

Span of rigging.—Is the length of the shrouds from the dead-eyes to the mast-head and down the other side.

Spar.—The term for any kind of mast, boom, &c.

Spar buoys.—A buoy showing only a mast above water.

Spar deck.—Defined as being the third deck from below. But the term is now used without much attention to the old meaning. It is best, perhaps, to define it as a light deck fitted over the upper deck of a vessel.

Spar-decked.—This term is applied to iron steamers whose sheer-strake plate is half above and half below the line of main deck beams.

Spar down.—This is to place spars in the rigging for the men to stand on whilst rattling down.

Sparred.—A vessel is lightly or heavily sparred according as her masts and yards are below or above her dimensions in weight and height.

Speaking.—A vessel is said to *speak*, when she begins to throw the water from her bows. Also, speaking is to meet and hail a ship at sea or to signal her with flags.

Speaking-trumpet.—A tube for hailing and speaking through, when the ship to be spoken is too far off for the natural voice to make itself heard. It is also used for issuing commands in a storm.

Spectioneer.—The head or chief harpooner in a whaler.

Spell.—An interval of labour or rest. As, to take a spell at the pumps is to be actively employed; to take a spell below, is to turn in and do nothing.

Spenser.—A try-sail.

Spent shot.—A shot near the end of its journey, but very capable of doing a deal of mischief.

Spewing oakum.—This is said of a vessel when through her labouring she forces the oakum out of her seams.

Spherical buoy.—A buoy showing a domed top above water.

Spider.—An iron outrigger to keep a block clear of the ship's side.

Spider-hoop.—A hoop round a mast fitted with belaying-pins.

Spilling-line.—A rope for shaking the wind out of a sail by spilling it.

Spinnaker.—A large triangular sail used by racing yachts.

Spinnaker boom.—A boom to extend a spinnaker sideways when the wind is abaft.

Spirketting.—The planking over the water-ways.

Spitfire jib.—A small yacht's jib made of strong canvas for rough weather.

Splice.—A connexion formed by passing the ends of two ropes through their strands.

Splice the main brace.—An expression to denote serving out grog.

"Splice the standing, knot the running rigging."—The method of temporarily repairing injuries sustained by the rigging after an engagement.

Sponsons.—Platforms or extensions on either side the paddle-box of a steamer.

Spoon-barge.—A barge furnished with an apparatus that lifts mud for dredging or cleansing purposes, and throws it into the bottom of the barge.

Spoon-drift.—A name given to the spray swept in a gale from the tops of seas and that forms a haze.

Spooning.—Running under small canvas. A very old and obsolete word.

Spread-eagle.—The posture of a man seized up to be flogged. To "make a spread-eagle" of a man is to flog him. "Brought to the gangway" means the same thing.

Spring.—A rope led from a ship's quarter to her cable, to bring her broadside to bear upon a given object. Also a rise or curve in the bow or stem of a ship.

Spring-stay.—A preventer stay for the extra support of a mast.

Spring tides.—High tides which occur after new and full moon.

Sprit.—A small sail carried by open boats. Also a sail carried by a barge called a spritsail barge.

Spritsail sheet-knot.—"No larger than a spritsail sheet-knot," said of a small man or boy.

Spritsail topsail.—A sail that formerly extended above the sprit sail by a yard which hung under the jib boom.

Spritsail-yard.—A yard that formerly crossed the lower part of the bowsprit on which a sail called the spritsail was set. The spritsail was furnished with a large hole at each lower corner to let the water escape. The spritsail-yard was retained long after the sail was disused, but is now almost universally replaced by *whiskers* (which see).

Spritsail-yard fore and aft.—In former times, when men-of-war were rigged with these spars upon their bowsprits, they would, before boarding an enemy, haul the spritsail yards round on a line, or nearly so, with the bowsprit, so that they might not be in the way. This was called "spritsail-yard fore and aft."

Spritsail-yarding.—Rigging a shark with a piece of spar through his nose and sending him adrift.

Sproket wheel.—A wheel in the chain-pump worked by a handle.

Sprung.—A spar is *sprung* when the fibres of the wood are injured by straining.

Spuds.—Jack's name for potatoes.

Spume.—Froth blown up by the wind. Very different from spray.

Spun-yarn.—Stuff made by twisting old yarns together with a little winch.

Spurling-line.—This used to be a line that was fitted to the wheel and an indicator to show the direction of the tiller.

Squall.—A sudden burst of wind of short duration; though, to be sure, a gale may sometimes come on in a squall.

Square.—Square-rigged, having yards instead of gaffs.

Square-butted.—This term is applied to a yard-arm sufficiently stout to enable a sheave-hole to be cut in it without weakening the spar.

Square knot.—A reef knot.

Square-rigged.—A ship; but the term is applied to any mast that carries square yards, such, for instance, as a brigantine, which you would describe as being *square-rigged* forward.

Square sail.—A large sail that is set from the deck upon the foreyard of a schooner.

Square-tucks.—Sterns square below, like boat's sterns, with a modern stern built up from the counter.

Square yards.—Literally when the yards lie fair upon the masts exactly athwartships, but the term is also applied to very or long yards.

Squaring-marks.—Marks on the lifts and braces for squaring the yards.

Squaring-yard signals.—A method of directing the bracing and topping of the yards by exhibiting hand-flags.

Squat.—A vessel is said to squat when she sails on an uneven keel.

Squatter.—To lie broad upon the water.

Squillagee.—A small swab.

Stabber.—A small marline-spike.

Staff.—A flag-pole.

Staff-captain.—A master of the fleet.

Staff-commander.—A master of fifteen years' seniority.

Stage.—A platform hung over the side for men to stand on whilst painting, carpentering, &c.

Staith.—A structure for shooting coal into a ship's hold.

Stanchion.—An upright support, such as the bulwark stanchions, the stanchions in a cabin, &c.

Standard.—A knee above the deck.

Standard compass.—A compass from which a ship's course is given and referred to the steering compass by comparison.

Standards.—Iron connexions between the stern-post and deck-beams of a screw-steamer to resist the vibration caused by the propeller.

Stand by!—An order to make ready. Literally, stand by the ropes, ready to let go.

Stand-by steering gear.—A wheel situated aft, working the rudder by screw-gear, for use in case of the midship steering-gear breaking down.

Standing.—Steering in a certain direction, as "she was standing to the eastward." Also, the part of a rope that is fast, that cannot be hauled on is called the standing part.

Standing gaff.—A gaff that does not lower, such as the gaff of a ship's mizzen which is taken in by being hauled down the gaff and brailed up against the mast.

Standing jib.—A large jib carried by ships or barques, but now replaced by the inner and outer jibs.

Standing rigging.—All the ropes in a ship which are fitted and stationary, such as the shrouds, stays and backstays, martingale, bobstays, &c.

Stands.—The name given to poles placed across rivers to bar entrance.

Starboard.—The right hand side, looking forward.

Starboard tack.—A ship is on this tack when she is sailing with the wind blowing over the right-hand bow.

Starboard the helm!—An order to shift the wheel so as to force the vessel's head to the left.

Starbowlines.—An old name for the portion of the crew who form the starboard watch.

Star-gazer.—An imaginary sail, like sky-scraper (which see).

Start.—Any fixed thing forcibly moved without being wholly removed from its place, as from the blow of a sea or a collision, is said to be started. Also a cask is said to be *started* when it is opened.

Starting gear.—The general name of the levers, wheels, &c., used for starting marine engines.

Station staffs.—Curved battens used in ship-building.

Stations for stays!—In a man-of-war this means to make ready for going about.

Staves.—The pieces of wood which form the sides of a cask.

Stay.—A rope that supports a mast by leading forward. The stays take their names from the masts they support, such as the main stay, the fore-topmast stay, the mizzen-topgallant stay.

Stayed forward or aft.—Said of masts inclined towards the bows or the stern by ill-judged tension of the stays or backstays.

Staying.—Tacking. The act of beating or going about.

Stays.—A vessel is in stays when she is in the act of tacking. It includes the whole procedure from the time of "helm's alee!" to "let go and haul!"

Stay-sail.—A fore-and-aft sail that hoists upon a stay. Stay-sails take their names from the stays on which they travel.

Stay-tackles.—Tackles attached to a stay for hoisting weights or lowering them.

Steady!—An order to the helmsman to keep the vessel heading as she goes.

Steadying-lines.—Ropes used in a boat for keeping her upright in hoisting.

Stealer.—The name given to a plank in a strake that does not extend right forward or aft.

Steam-chest.—A term that indicates the space above the water-surface in the boiler of a marine engine.

Steam-circle.—A circle drawn on the chart round the port to which a steamer is bound, for calculating distance with reference to the amount of coal on board.

Steam-gauge.—An indicator for showing the pressure in pounds of steam upon the square inch in boilers.

Steam-pipe.—A pipe connected with the stop or communication valve of a marine boiler to convey the steam to the super heater or from one boiler to another or to the engines.

Steam-space.—The portion of the boiler, above the water-level, where the steam accumulates.

Steam-steering apparatus.—A helm that is governed by steam. A man revolves the wheel, but the steam-engine turns the rudder. There are many different sorts.

Steeple engine.—The name given to a marine engine whose guide to the connecting-rod works above the crank shaft.

Steep-tub.—A tub in which salt meat is soaked to freshen it.

Steerage.—The after interior of a ship under the saloon, if she has a poop. By some the steerage of a ship is apparently considered to be wherever her steerage passengers are lodged. The term, however, sufficiently indicates the right locality.

Steerage-way.—Said of a vessel that has just movement enough to answer her helm.

Steer-oar.—An oar used in steering a boat.

Steeve.—A bowsprit steeves more or less according to the angle it makes with the horizon. Also to stow freight, from *stevedore* (which see).

Stemson.—A timber used as a support for the stem.

Step.—A timber on which the heel of a mast rests.

Stern-all!—An order to rowers to back the boat.

Sternboard.—Making a ship go backwards by her sails.

Stern chaser.—A gun in the stern-port of a ship for firing at an enemy in the wake.

Stern-on.—Keeping the stern of a boat at the seas rolling after her. Also said of a ship that rounds and presents her stern as she recedes.

Stern-ports.—Ports between the stern timbers for lights, ventilation, &c. Also for guns.

Stern-sheets.—The after-part of an open boat.

Stern-tube.—A cylinder in the after peak of a steamer in which the propeller shaft works.

Stern-tube bulkhead.—A division at the foremost end of the lazarette, to prevent the water from entering the hold should any accident befall the propeller or shaft.

Stern-walk.—In the days of three-deckers this was a platform or gallery over the stern.

Stern-way.—The movement of a vessel carried or impelled backwards.

Stevedore.—A man who stows cargo in a ship under the captain's order.

Steward.—A saloon waiter. One who has charge of the stores. Those under him are called under-stewards.

Sticks.—A name given to masts. "She has handsome sticks," that is, she is handsomely sparred.

Stiff.—A term applied to a ship when she is able to bear a press of sail without heeling over to any great extent.

Stiffening-booms.—Booms used for steadying vessels from which the ballast has been removed, thus enabling them to be moved to their loading berths.

Stink-pot.—A contrivance thrown on an enemy's deck. It gives forth a horrid smell. It is still used by Chinese pirates.

Stirrups.—Pieces of rope to support the foot-ropes, or rather, on long yards, to prevent the foot-ropes from making so deep a bight as to bring a man too low for working when standing on them.

Stock.—The cross piece on the upper part of the shank of an anchor.

Stockade.—Timbers joined by iron chains and strengthened by a cable twisted round them and mounted at each end with cannons. An old method of fortifying the mouth of a river.

Stocker-bait.—Small fish given by smack-owners to their apprentices to sell for their own profit.

Stocks.—A fabric of shores and blocks shelving towards the water in which ships are built.

Stock tackle and pendent.—A tackle for dragging in the upper arm of the anchor stock.

Stoke-hole.—A place in a steamer occupied by the men who feed the fires.

Stoker.—A trimmer or fireman who attends to a steamer's furnaces.

Stools.—Small channels for the dead-eyes of the backstays. Also supports for the shaft bearings of a propeller-shaft.

Stop.—A fastening of small stuff. See Stopping.

Stop!—The cry in heaving the log. It is delivered by the person who holds the sand-glass to denote that the sand has run out and that the log-line must be checked.

Stop-cock.—A cock for shutting off communication between boilers.

Stoppage in transitu.—A term signifying that an unpaid seller or consigner of goods has a right, on the insolvency of the purchaser or consignee, to stop delivery of those goods.

Stopper.—To pass a stopper is a method of securing a rope whilst it is being made fast.

Stopper-bolts.—Ring-bolts for the deck stoppers.

Stopping.—Fastening two parts of a rope together by binding them side by side.

Stop-valves.—A valve affixed to the upper part of a boiler for confining the steam or letting it into the steam-pipes leading to the engines. Also used for letting steam from one boiler into another.

Stop-water.—A plug driven into the scarph [or scarf; a type of woodworking joint] of a keel or the foot of the stem or stern-post to prevent the water from finding its way into the ship.

Storage.—Charges for storing articles of merchandise in dock accommodation.

Store-rooms.—Rooms in a man-of-war where the carpenter's, gunner's and boatswain's stores are kept.

Storm-disk.—The thin whirling stratum of air that constitutes the cyclone.

Storm-finch.—A name for the petrel or Mother Carey's chickens.

Storm-jib.—A fore-and-aft sail of stout canvas used by ships in heavy weather.

Storm-sails.—Sails of No. 1 canvas, bent for use in stormy latitudes.

Strand.—A number of yarns twisted and forming a part of a rope.

Stranded.—The situation of a vessel when ashore.

Stranger.—This name is given to a vessel that heaves in sight showing no colours, and of which no particulars can be ascertained.

Stray line.—About sixty or seventy feet of the log-line next the log-ship for paying overboard, so that the log-ship may go clear of the eddy.

Streak or **strake**.—A range of plates or planks along a ship's side.

Stream a buoy.—Is to drop it overboard.

Stream anchor.—An anchor in size between the bower and the kedge. It is used for warping and sometimes for mooring.

Streamer.—A pennant.

Stream-ice.—The name given to ice when drifting along in a narrow line.

Stretch.—A board. A long stretch is to sail a long distance on one tack.

Stretchers.—Supports for the feet at the bottom of a boat for rowing. Also supports placed between the sides of a boat when hoisted and griped. Also yarns full of exaggeration or downright lies.

Stretch out!—An order to rowers to bend their backs.

Strike.—To submit to a conqueror by hauling down the colours.

Striking a mast.—Is to send it down on deck.

Stringers are of two kinds: hold and deck stringers. The deck-stringer is a strake of plating to stiffen the bottom plating, &c.; hold-stringers are connected to the bottom and riveted to alternate frames. They serve as strong internal fastenings in iron and wooden ships.

Stroke.—A single sweep of an oar through the water. Also the person who pulls the stroke or aftermost oar.

Stroke-side.—The side of a boat where the aftermost oar ships.

Strop.—Literally a strap. A ring of rope or iron round a block.

Studding-sails.—Sails extended beyond the usual square sails. They are hoisted by halliards leading through jewel-blocks at the yard-arms, and are extended at the foot by studding-sail booms. On the fore are the lower, topmast, and topgallant studding-sails: on the main, topmast and topgallant studding-sails. Royal studding-sails are sometimes carried.

Studding-sail boom.—A spar that rigs in and out upon a lower top-sailor topgallant yard for stretching the foot of a studding-sail upon.

Studding-sail yard.—The spar to which the head of a studding-sail is attached.

Studs.—Pieces of iron across the middle of the links of a chain cable.

Stuff.—A word to denote small lines, yarns, &c., for seizing, serving, and the like.

Stuffing-box.—A means of packing the piston of an engine to keep it steam-tight.

Stump topgallant mast.—Topgallant masts without royal masts above them. They are also called short topgallant masts.

Stun'sail.—Sailor's pronunciation of studding-sail.

Sub-lieutenant.—A midshipman of the Royal Navy who has passed for lieutenant.

Sucking-pump.—A pump that raises water by exhausting the air in the pump barrel.

Suction pipes.—Pipes in a steamer for pumping the vessel out by the engines. They lead from the different compartments to the engine-room, and are, or should be, connected not only to the bilge-pumps on the main engines, but to the donkey pumps.

Sue.—When a ship is ashore, she is said to *sue* as the water leaves her.

Sugg.—To rock with the action of the sea when stranded.

Suit of canvas.—All the sails required to be bent, but not the spare sails.

Sumatras.—Winds encountered in the Straits of Malacca.

Sumner's method.—A mode of finding out a ship's position at sea when the latitude is doubtful or the chronometer inaccurate.

Sun dog.—A mock sun shining near the sun.

Sun-swing.—A term signifying the influence of the sun in its to-and-fro motion between the Tropics upon the polar limits of the trade-winds.

Supercargo.—A person in a merchant-ship who manages the sales and superintends the commercial part of a voyage.

Super-heater.—A contrivance, variously constructed, placed in the up-take of a marine steam-engine, to increase the heat of the steam in its passage from the boiler to the engine.

Supper.—Tea is called supper at sea, being the last meal. A sailor never "drinks tea," but "gets his supper."

Supporter.—A knee bolted to the side of a ship and the cathead.

Surface-condenser.—A method of condensing steam from the cylinder of a marine engine, whereby the condensed steam returns to the boiler as pure water.

Surge.—A wave. Also to yield, to give, or to payout, as surge the cable.

Surging.—The slipping of the cable round the windlass barrel, or of a hawser or rope round the barrel of a capstan.

Survey.—Observations, soundings, &c., for the construction of charts.

Surveyors.—Persons employed by the Board of Trade and Lloyd's. The duty of the officers of the Board of Trade is to see that ships are seaworthy: that of the latter to see that they are built in accordance with Lloyd's rules for classification. The former are supposed to act in the interests of human life, the others in the interest of property.

Swab.—An epaulette. Also a mop composed of rope-yarns used for drying the decks. Also a term of contempt when applied to a man.

Swallow.—The part of a block through which the rope reeves.

Swatchway.—An opening in a shoal. A narrow, navigable by small vessels, in a sand-bank.

Sway away!—An order to haul aloft, to hoist up.

Swear through a nine-inch plank.—An old sea-term expressive of a man who would swear to any lie. It was a favourite expression of Lord Nelson when referring to American skippers.

Sweating cargo.—A cargo, such as wool, that exudes and produces an atmosphere obnoxious to health, and susceptible of spontaneous ignition.

Sweating the purser.—An old term for wasting ship's stores.

Sweeps.—Long, heavy oars.

Swell.—The heaving of the sea.

Swifter.—The forward shroud of a lower mast. Also a rope for keeping a capstan bar to its place when inserted in the capstan.

Swifter in.—To tauten slack standing rigging by bringing the opposite shrouds together.

Swig.—To drink. Also to haul taut.

Swing the monkey.—A game that consists in striking with knotted handkerchiefs a man who swings to a rope made fast aloft. The person the "monkey" strikes whilst swinging, takes his place.

Swinging-boom.—A boom at a ship's side that extends the foot of a lower studding-sail.

Swinging-tray.—A tray in a cabin or saloon depending from the ceiling or deck. These trays are usually placed over the tables, so that glasses, decanters, &c., may be placed upon them. They swing with the roll of the ship, and thus prevent the things they support from capsizing.

Swing off.—To pull upon a taut rope at right angles. Also *swig off*.

Swipes.—The washings and rinsings of old beer barrels.

Swivel.—A revolving link of a chain cable. Every *length* of cable is swivelled. See Cable.

Sword mat.—A mat used as chafing gear.

Sympiesometer.—An instrument for measuring the weight of the atmosphere. It is used with the barometer whose indications it forestalls.

T

Tabernacle.—A wooden box, hollow above the deck and then solid to the bottom of the vessel. The mast steps in it, and is secured by a pin. The back is open, so that the mast can be lowered. When the mast is erect the tabernacle is closed by a clamp.

Table-cloth.—A white cloud that sometimes covers the top of Table Mountain, Cape of Good Hope.

Table-money.—An allowance to admirals and senior officers, outside their pay, for purposes of official hospitality.

Tabling.—The double part of a sail close to the bolt-rope.

Taboo.—A custom in the South Sea Islands. A piece of white tappa is fastened to a ship's jib boom, as a sign that the vessel must not be boarded by the islanders. A ship so decorated is said to be under a taboo.

Tack.—The rope attached to the weather corner of a course. The foremost lower corner of a fore-and-aft sail.

Tack-block.—A block fitted at the outer end of a topgallant and main-topmast studding-sail boom.

Tacking.—Beating against the wind.

Tackle.—A purchase formed of a rope rove through blocks.

Tack-pins.— Also called jack-pins, belaying-pins.

Tack (to).—To beat, to go about, to reach.

Tail.—A rope at the end of a block for attaching it to anything.

Tail-block.—A block with a short length of rope spliced into the end.

Tail-jigger.—A tackle composed of a double and single block.

Tail of a gale.—The close of a gale.

Tail on!—An order to lay hold and pull. More often "tally on."

Tail tackle.—A watch-tackle.

Taking a departure.—See Departure.

Tallow down.—To coat over the bright work of an engine with a mixture of white lead and tallow.

Tally.—To check freight going over the side in board or out.

Tallyman.—The person who tallies.

Tally on.—An order to catch hold and haul.

Tangent screw.—A screw for perfecting the contact of the index of a sextant.

Tap the admiral.—Said of a man who would drink anything.

Tartar.—A lateen-rigged vessel with one mast.

Tatoo.—Blue or red devices pricked into the flesh of seamen.

Taunt.—Tall.

Taut.—Tight.

Taut hand.—The term for an officer severe in his discipline.

Taut leech.—Said of a sail on a wind when well set.

Tea chop.—A lighter in which tea for freight is brought alongside ships in China.

Tea wagon.—Formerly an East Indiaman.

Tell-tale.—An inverted compass fixed in a cabin.

Tend.—To watch a vessel at anchor as the tide turns, so as to keep her cables clear.

Tender.—A vessel waiting on another or others. A ship is said to be tender when she heels easily under a weight of wind.

Tenon.—The heel of a mast that fits into the step.

Terre Altos.—N.W. squalls encountered in the neighbourhood of Rio de Janeiro.

Test-cock.—A small cock fitted to the feed-pipe of a marine engine between the valve chest and boiler for drawing off feed water to test temperature.

There she breezes!—An exclamation used when the wind freshens and the ship drives through it at an increased speed.

Thermometer.—An instrument for showing the temperature of the air.

Thick and thin block.— Having one sheave larger than the other.

Thick-stuff.—An old author defines this term as "all plank which is thicker than four inches."

Thimble.—An iron eye or ring grooved to receive a rope.

Thin waterway.—The deck-plank nearest to the waterway, and that follows the curve of the ship's side.

Thole-mat.—A mat for muffling the sound of oars in the pins.

Thole-pins.—Pieces of wood fitted into the gunwale of a boat to steady the oars in rowing.

Thorough footing.—Passing the end of a rope through its own coil and then taking it to the capstan for a stretching.

Three-decker.—A ship with three whole battery decks.

Three-flag signals.—Three flags hoisted in alphabetical order and meant to represent questions and replies on general matters.

Throat.—The inner corner of a spanker or stay-sail.

Throat halliards.—Halliards to hoist a gaff.

Throat seizing.—A seizing for block strops, &c.

Throttle valve.—A valve in the throat of the steam-pipe next to the cylinder for regulating the supply of steam.

Through the fleet.—An abolished punishment that consisted in towing a culprit through a fleet of vessels at each one of which he received a certain number of lashes.

Thrum.—To make a rough surface on a mat by inserting short strands of yarn.

Thwart.—A seat in an open boat.

Thwart-ships.—Crosswise.

Tic-a-tack.—A Chinese boat like a sampan.

Tide.—The regular rising and falling of the waters of the ocean.

Tide-rip.—A disturbance in mid-ocean caused by the meeting of two currents.

Tide-rode.—Swung by the force of the tide.

Tide sail.—"A captain on a tide sail," that is, a captain ready to leave dock by the next tide.

Tier.—A range of casks. The range of the bights of a cable.

Tierce.—A cask of beef.

Tight.—Said of a vessel free from leaks. Also said of a man intoxicated.

Tiller.—A piece of timber or metal fitted upon the rudder-head fore-and-aft and used for steering.

Tiller-head.—The extremity of the tiller to which the wheel-chains are attached.

Tiller-ropes.—Ropes used before the adoption of wheel-chains, leading from the tiller-head round the barrel of the wheel.

Tilt.—A boat canopy.

Timber.—A term for all large pieces of wood.

Timber-heads.—The tops of the timbers above the decks.

Timber-hitch.—A rope passed round a spar, &c., and the end passed round and under its own part.

Timber-pond.—A space of water in the vicinity of docks for the convenience of storing timber.

Timbers.—The ribs of a wooden ship.

Time-ball.—A ball dropped in accurate correspondence with Greenwich time.

Timenoguy.—A rope to prevent the sheet or tack of a course from fouling in working.

Timoneer.—The helmsman.

Tipping the grampus.—Ducking a man for sleeping in his watch on deck.

Tip the nines.—To founder by being overset from press of canvas.

Toe a line!—Stand in a row.

Togged to the nines.—In full rig and dressed with uncommon care.

Toggle.—A pin through any kind of eye to prevent it from drawing out of its place.

Toggle-bolt.—For holding a small flag-staff by means of a strap.

Togs.—Clothes.

Tomahawk.—A kind of pole-axe that was formerly used by boarders.

Tom Cox's traverse.—"Tom Cox's traverse, three turns round the long boat and a pull at the scuttle butt," said of a man who shirks work, feigns to be busy in doing nothing, &c.

Tommy.—Bread.

Tom Pepper.—A liar.

Tompion.—A plug in a cannon's mouth.

Tonnage-deck.—The upper deck in ships which have less than three decks, and the second deck from below in all other ships.

Top.—A platform on each lower mast, to spread the top-mast rigging and for men to stand on in working aloft.

Top-awnings.—Hammocks in the rigging, stowed there to protect the men in the top.

Top-blocks.—Large single iron-bound blocks used for sending topmasts up or down.

Top-board.—A board formerly affixed to the after-side of tops and variously ornamented.

Top-burton.—A tackle composed of a double block fitted with a hook, and a single block fitted with a hook and thimble, whilst a long strop with a thimble at the end is fitted to the strop of the single block.

Top-castles.—Anciently the tops of ships.

Tope.—A small junk.

Topgallant breeze.—A wind not so strong but that a ship can show her main-topgallant sail to it.

Topgallant forecastle.—A raised structure on the forecastle of a ship, in which the crew sleep.

Topgallant sheets are flown!—Formerly a signal to intimate that an enemy was in sight.

Top-light.—A signal lantern on an admiral's ship.

Top-lining.—A lining to prevent the after-part of a top-sail from chafing against the rim of the top.

Top-maul.—A large hammer used by riggers.

Top-men.—In a man-of-war hands stationed in the tops for working the upper sails.

Topping.—Boot-topping is cleansing a vessel's bottom, and then smearing it with grease, &c.

Topping-lift.—A rope used for lifting up the end of a boom.

Top-rail.—A rail across the hinder part of a top.

Top-sail haul!—An order in tacking when the main-sail is furled.

Topsail sheet-block.—A block shackled or stropped into the clew of a top-sail for bending the sheets.

Top-swivel.—A small gun formerly worked in a ship's tops.

Top the glim.—Snuff a candle.

Top-timbers.—The highest timbers on a vessel's side.

Top up.—To raise a boom with the topping-lift.

Tormentor.—A fork used in fishing out the salt meat from the coppers.

Tornadoes.—Furious gusts of wind which blow from all parts of the horizon, chiefly encountered off the Guinea coast.

Tosher.—A small fishing-vessel.

Toss.—To throw up an oar and lay it down with its blade forward.

Tot.—A small measure. A tot of grog was the dose served out at the quarter-deck capstan in the days of grog at sea.

Tot of grog.—A gill of rum.

Touch.—A sail *touches* when it is brought so close to the wind that its weather leech shakes.

Touch her up.—Shake a vessel by luffing.

Touching.—Touching the wind is sailing so close as to keep the upper leeches lifting.

Touching at.—Anchoring or putting into a port during a voyage.

Tow.—To draw, to tug.

Towing-bridle.—A chain to attach a hawser to for towing.

Tow-rail.—The arched rail on the after-part of a tug upon which the towing hawser travels or rests.

Town-ho!—An old whaling cry raised by the masthead-man on first sighting a whale.

"To work hard, live hard, die hard, and go to hell after all would be hard indeed!"—Jack's philosophy.

T-plates.—Irons under a ship's channels for extra strength.

Trade-room.—A Yankee name for a part of the hold where fancy goods for barter, &c., are kept.

Trade-winds.—Winds which prevail in the Atlantic and Pacific Oceans, between the limits of about 30° N. and S. latitude. On the N. side of the Equator the winds are called the N.E. Trades, on the S. side the S.E. Trades.

Trail-boards.—Ornamental boards on either side a ship's stern.

Training-ship.—A ship for the training of boys for the navy and merchant-service.

Train-tackle.—A tackle for running guns in and out.

Trammel.—A net for river and sea work.

Transient ships.—Merchant-vessels which are neither liners nor regular traders; the term signifies that they are at one place to-day and somewhere else to-morrow.

Transoms.—Timbers across a ship's stern for receiving the ends of deck planks, &c.

Transom stern.—The old-fashioned square stern.

Transport.—A ship that conveys troops.

Trapping-lines.—Lines passed round the hawsers from the quarters of a vessel having another in tow, to prevent the ends from getting foul of the propeller, should the hawsers part.

Traps.—A sailor's *traps* are his clothes, bedding, chest, &c. When he talks of going ashore with his traps, these are the things he means.

Traveller.—An iron ring to slip along a rope.

Traverse a yard.—Getting it fore-and-aft.

Traverse-board.—A board for indicating a ship's course, by pegs inserted in holes.

Traverse-sailing.—A method in navigation of reducing the zigzag track of a ship into a single course and distance.

Traverse tables.—Tables used for a variety of calculations in navigation and chiefly for working out the dead reckoning.

Trawler.—A smack that fishes by shooting a trawl-net.

Trawl-warp.—A warp about 60 fathoms long, used by smacks in towing the trawl.

Treble-reefed.—Said of a top-sail with three reefs tied in it.

Treenails.—Long wooden pegs for fastening planking to timber, &c.

Trend.—The direction pursued by a coast. Also the lower end of the shank of an anchor.

Trestle-trees.—Fore-and-aft pieces on each side a mast to support the cross-trees and top.

Triatic stay.—A rope at the heads of the fore and main masts, fitted with thimbles to hook the stay-tackles to.

Trice.—To haul up.

Trick.—Two hours at the helm.

Trim.—The condition of a vessel with reference to her posture on the water. To trim a vessel is to adjust her posture afloat by the head or stern.

Trimmer.—A man employed in loading coal.

Trimming.—A beating or jacketting.

Trip.—To raise an anchor off the ground.

Tripping.—Lifting a mast to withdraw the fid.

Tripping-line.—For tripping a royal or topgallant yard in sending it down.

Trip-stopper.—A short chain secured by eyebolts to the side, and used for canting the anchor in letting go.

Tropics.—Are contained within the parallels of latitude 23°28′ north and south of the Equator.

Trow.—A kind of barge.

Truck.—A round piece of wood at the head of the highest mast, with two holes, through which the flag-halliards are rove.

Trundle-shot.—A bolt of iron, pointed and furnished with balls of lead.

Trunk engine.—A marine engine furnished with a cylindrical casing fastened to the upper part of the piston, and constructed to slide steam-tight through the cylinder cover.

Trunk hatchway.—A hatchway framed down to a lower deck and presenting the appearance of a shaft.

Trunnions.—Arms of a gun, which serve as an axle for its depression or elevation.

Truss.—An iron crutch to keep a lower yard close to the mast.

Truss-strops.—Chain strops lashed on top of the yard for the truss pendants to shackle to.

Try-sail.—A fore-and-aft sail setting on a gaff.

Try-sail mast.—A small mast abaft a lower mast for hoisting a trysail on.

Try-work.—Large iron pots, used in whalers, built in brick-work and supported by stanchions.

Tub.—Grog-tub, for spirits; halliard-tub, for coiling away topsail halliards; match-tub, formerly for protecting the slow-match in an engagement.

Tubes.—Pipes connected with a steamer's engines, through which the heat and flames pass, and which heat the water that surrounds them. Sometimes water is in the tubes and the heat outside.

Tubular boiler.—A marine boiler furnished with numerous tubes, surrounded with water, through which the flame and hot gases from the furnaces are led to the up-take at the bottom of the chimney.

Tuck.—The ends of the after-planks under the counter.

Tug.—A steamboat used for towing vessels.

Tumble up!—A cry to the men to bear a hand in coming on deck.

Tumbling home.—The depression inwards of a ship's sides above the bends.

Tunnel.—A hollow space in screw steamers, extending from under the engine-room to the stern-tube bulkhead, in which the propeller shaft works, and meant to enable it to be inspected.

Turn.—To take a turn is to pass a rope once or twice round a pin or kevel.

Turn and turn about.—Alternate duty, one resting whilst the other works.

Turn in.—To go to bed.

Turn in a dead-eye.—To secure by seizing the end of a shroud or stay round a dead-eye.

Turning out reefs.—Shaking out reefs, unknotting the reef-points to enlarge the sail.

Turn in rigging.—Taking the ends of the shrouds round the dead-eyes and securing them by seizings.

Turn out.—To get up out of bed.

Turnpike sailors.—Sham seamen who beg under pretence of having been shipwrecked.

Turn-table.—An apparatus for transferring a gun from one port to another. Also in a dock for transferring timber from ships into sheds.

Turn the hands up.—An order for all hands.

Turn to.—To go to work. To fall to. A favourite expression of sailors: "To turn to and do such and such a thing."

Turn turtle.—To capsize.

Turn up.—"Turn the hands up," send or call the men up from below.

Turret.—A massive iron structure on the deck of an ironclad man-of-war, rising some feet above the breastwork, and furnished with machinery for working the large guns mounted in it.

Turret-ship.—A vessel furnished with revolving turrets fitted with ordnance of the heaviest class.

Twiddling-line.—A rope for steadying the wheel.

Twigging-line.—A line attached to the bowl of a compass to remedy its sluggishness by twitching.

Twig the fore.—Seeing that all the sails are properly furled and the yards square forward. "Twig the main" is the same thing, referring to the main-mast.

Twine.—Fine small stuff made from hemp, used in sail-making.

Twin-screw.—A vessel fitted with two propellers worked by separate engines.

Twin-ship.—A vessel formed of two hulls. The idea is as old as 1663, in which year Sir William Petty invented a double-bottomed ship that proved a failure.

Two bowlines.—A term in fleet manoeuvres, applied when the ships of each column are ranged on each quarter of a single ship.

Two deck.—A ship with two whole battery decks.

Tye or tie.—A chain or rope attached to a yard for hoisting.

Typhoons.—Furious winds encountered in the China and Arabian Seas.

U

Unbend.—To untie. To remove a sail from a yard or a stay, &c.

Unbitt.—To remove the turns of a cable from the bitts.

Under canvas.—Said of a steamer using her sails only.

Under command.—Said of a ship over which there is control of the helm.

Under-manned.—Insufficiently furnished with men.

Under-masted.—Said of a ship whose spars are too small and short.

Under the lee.—In shelter from the wind by the shore or any other thing.

Under tow.—The back-wash of water in a recoiling breaker.

Under way.—Said of a ship that has just started after getting her anchor.

Underwriter.—One who takes the risk of insurance, and writes his name at the foot of the policy.

Union down.—The English ensign inverted: a distress signal.

Union Jack.—The union used separately.

Unmoor.—To get in one anchor that the vessel may ride by one only.

Unrove his life-line.—Said of a man who has died.

Unship.—To remove.

Up anchor!—The order to man the windlass.

Up and down.—A tackle consisting of a double block with a lashing and a single block with a hook.

Up boats.—The order to hoist the boats to the davits.

Up keeleg.—An expression signifying the act of starting to run away.

Up making.—Pieces of timber for filling up in building.

Upper counter rail.—A projecting moulding on the stern of a ship.

Upper deck.—The topmost deck of a three-decked ship.

Upper fore-topgallant sail.—The topmost half of a fore-topgallant sail divided by a yard.

Upper fore-topsail.—The portion of the fore-topsail that is next the topgallant sail.

Upper main-topgallant sail.—The topmost half of a main-topgallant sail divided by a yard.

Upper main-topsail.—The portion of the main-topsail that is next to the topgallant sail.

Upper masts.—The masts above the lower masts.

Upper mizzen-topsail.—The portion of the sail next to the topgallant sail.

Upper works.—The fabric of a ship above water.

Up-take.—A portion of the boiler through which the smoke and heat pass into the funnel after they have left the tubes.

Up with the helm.—Put it so as to bring the rudder to leeward of the stern-post.

V

Valued policy.—A policy of marine insurance wherein the value insured is named.

Van.—The foremost ships of a fleet.

Vane.—See Dog-vane.

Vane-spindle.—A spindle at the masthead on which the dog-vane works.

Vangee.—An apparatus consisting of a barrel and crank breaks for pumping a ship.

Vangs.—Ropes used for steadying a gaff.

Variation.— Variation of the compass is the deviation of the points of the compass from the corresponding points of the horizon. It is termed east or west variation, according as the north point of the compass is inclined from the true north.

'Vast.—Stop, as 'vast heaving.

Veer.—The wind veers when it shifts from right to left, or with the sun. To slack out cable.

Veer and haul.—Said of a shifting wind. Also a method of pulling on a rope.

Vent.—An aperture near the breech of a gun by which the charge is fired.

Vent-bit.—A tool for clearing the vent of a gun.

Vent-piece.— That which contains the vent in a breech-loading gun.

Vent-plug.—A plug for stopping the vent of a gun against wet, &c.

Veritas.—A register of shipping in Paris.

Vernier.—A small scale for moving up and down a barometer scale.

Vertex.—A term used by Raper, who defines it thus:—"When the course shaped on the great circle (Great Circle Sailing) from each point is less than 90° (reckoning both courses from the nearest pole) the circle passes through a point in a higher latitude than that of either of the places. The point of extreme latitude reached, at which the ship, neither increasing nor diminishing her latitude for a time, steers E. or W. we shall call the *Vertex*."

Vertical fire.—Firing at such an elevation that the projectile drops nearly plumb.

Vessel.—Any kind of ship.

V.G.—An endorsement signifying "very good" on a seaman's certificate of conduct.

Vice-Admiral.—The rank after an admiral, and indicated by a flag at the fore.

Victualling-bill.—A warrant obtained by a shipmaster to ship stores for the use of the crew and passengers, containing a statement of the stores.

Victualling yards.—Large repositories for marine stores, near the Royal Dockyards.

Viol.—A messenger used in weighing an anchor by a capstan. Formerly it was a large hawser.

Viol-block.—A large block, formerly used in weighing the anchor.

Virazon.—A S.E. wind veering to N.E. encountered in the neighbourhood of the Rio de la Plata.

Visitation and search.—The right of every belligerent cruiser to overhaul a merchantman.

Vitry.—Also **Vittory**. A light canvas.

Volley.—A simultaneous discharge of fire-arms.

Voluntary stranding.—Running a vessel ashore to escape foundering, or any other danger.

Voyage.—A journey by sea out and home.

W

Wad.—A plug for keeping a shot in its place when rammed home.

Waggoner.—A famous old atlas used by seamen in past times.

Waist.—The deck between the main deck and the forecastle.

Waist-boards.—Berthing in a vessel's gangways.

Waist-cloths.—Coverings for the hammocks stowed in the waist-nettings.

Waisters.—An old name for seamen or boys of little use.

Waist-nettings.—The hammock-nettings in the waist.

Wake.—The track left by a ship in motion.

Wales.—Planks running the whole length of a vessel's sides.

Walk back.—To reverse the action of the capstan so as to come up or ease the rope round it.

Walking the plank.—An old mode of murdering by forcing a man to step overboard from a plank.

Walk up Ladder-lane and down Hemp-street.—Said of a man hanged at a yard-arm.

Wall.—A knot on the end of a rope.

Wall-sided.—A term applied to the top sides of ships whose sides, when she is afloat, look to be up and down like a wall.

Wapp.—A fair-leader. Also a shroud-stopper.

Wardroom.—A cabin in a man-of-war where the commissioned officers mess.

Wardroom-officers.—The commander, lieutenant, master, chaplain, paymaster, surgeon, marine officers, and assistant-surgeons.

Warm-sided.—Said of a ship mounting heavy batteries.

Warp.—The name given to a rope for dragging a ship into any required position.

Warping.—The act of hauling a ship into a required position.

Warrant.—A dock-warrant is a document representing goods warehoused in a dock.

Warrant-officer.—In the navy, the boatswain, gunner, carpenter, &c.

Wash-boards.—Angular pieces of wood placed under the lower cheeks and eikings of a ship.

Wash down.—To clean the decks with water and scrubbing brushes.

Watch.—The term applied to the division of a crew. There are two watches, i.e. the *port watch* headed by the mate, and the *starboard watch* by the second mate.

Watch and watch.—The term to signify four hours on deck and four below, alternately, save in the dog-watches, which are two hours each.

Watch, ho, watch!—The cry of men heaving the deep-sea lead as the fakes of the line drop from their hands.

Watch-tackle.—A small handy purchase consisting of a tailed double-block and a single block with a hook.

Water-bailiff.—An officer for the searching of vessels.

Water-ballast.—A method of ballasting a vessel by filling specially constructed compartments or tanks with water.

Water bewitched.—The tea served out to sailors.

Water-borne.—Sustained by the water, lifted by a sea. Said of a boat hanging at the davits that she was water-borne by the heeling of the ship.

Water-gauge cocks.—Small cocks placed in front of a marine boiler, by opening which the height of the water in the boiler is ascertained.

Watering.—Filling a ship's tanks or casks with fresh water.

Water-line.—The line of flotation when a ship is loaded.

Water-logged.—A vessel full of water and floating on her cargo of timber, cork, or freight of that kind, is called water-logged.

Waterman.—This word is defined as one who gets his livelihood on fresh water; but it is generally used as another term for boatman, who rows for hire either on salt or fresh water.

Water-marks.—The figures on a ship's stern showing the depth of water she draws.

Water-pads.—Harbour thieves.

Water-ports.—Openings in a ship's bulwarks to free the deck of water.

Water-sail.—A sail set under the swinging boom when the lower studding-sail is set.

Water-space.—The term applied to the space for holding water, as, for instance, between the side of one furnace and the side of the shell of the boiler, or between the plates of the combustion chamber and the shell of the boiler.

Water-tables.—Sills to a ship's windows.

Water-tight bulkheads.—Divisions in iron steamships to prevent them from sinking through injury by collision or from springing a leak.

Water-ways.—The planking along the scuppers.

'Way aloft!—An order to go aloft for reefing, furling, &c.

Ways.—Timbers laid down for rolling weights upon.

Wearing.—To come round on another tack by passing stem to wind.

Weather.—To weather is to pass on the windward side of an object.

Weather-bitt.—That to which the weather-cable is secured when a ship is moored. Also to take an extra turn with a cable round the windlass end.

Weather-boards.—Protections for a ship's ports when laid up in ordinary.

Weather-bound.—Stopped by adverse winds.

Weather-cloths.—Hammock covers of tarpaulin or painted canvas.

Weather-glass.—The barometer.

Weather-lurch.—A strong roll to windward. Also termed *weather roll*.

Weatherly.—Said of a ship that looks well up into the wind when on a bowline.

Weatherly ship.—Said of a ship that makes little or no leeway in working to windward.

Weather scuppers.—It is an old joke at sea to advise a greenhorn to get a handspike and hold it down hard in the weather scuppers to steady the ship's wild motions.

Weather-side.—The side on which the wind blows.

Weather-tide.—A tide that sets the ship to windward.

Weather-wheel.—The side of the wheel on which the wind is blowing.

Wee-gee.—A method of working two pumps by long iron handles and ropes, instead of brakes.

Weevil.—A worm found in bad ship's-biscuit.

Weigh.—To lift.

Weighing.—Lifting the anchor off the ground.

Weight of metal.—The united calibres, in pounds, of all the gun which a ship can place in battery.

Well!—An exclamation, signifying that will do, as "Well the royal yard!" "Well the cross-jack yard!" Also a shaft that goes down to the keelson, used for sounding; and, in small smacks, a place in the hold into which the fish taken are thrown.

Well cabin.—An after cabin without windows.

Well-deck.—A vessel with a long poop and forecastle, and between, a deck made deep by high bulwarks, is called *well-decked*.

Well man.—A man who is in good health.

Wester.—To draw to the westwards, said of the sun or wind.

Westing.—The distance made by course to the westwards.

Wet.—A wet ship is a vessel which takes water over her easily.

Wet dock.—An excavation, contiguous to the water, for the accommodation of ships.

Wet provisions.—The term applied to beef, pork, vinegar, rum, lime-juice, and suet.

Wharfinger.—The owner or keeper of a wharf.

What cheer?—A nautical salutation, meaning "What news?" "What luck?"

Wheel.—A wheel with handles for revolving the ropes or chains which move the tiller or yoke in steering.

Wheel-house.—A cover over the wheel for the protection of the helmsman.

Wheel stanchion.—The supporter of the axle on which the wheel revolves.

Where away!—How does the object bear? How is it situated with reference to the ship?

Wherry.—A small open boat. Also a large barge or lighter.

While she creaks she holds!—An exclamation used as a kind of encouragement to persevere in keeping the ship under a press.

Whip-jack.—A sham sailor.

Whipping.—Preserving the end of a rope by binding it with twine.

Whipping baskets.—Baskets used for discharging certain kinds of cargo.

Whip upon whip.—A whip attached to the fall of another.

Whiskers.—Two booms or irons extending on either side a ship's head for guying the jib booms.

Whistling-buoy.—A floating-fog signal, consisting of a buoy whose movements operate a whistle.

White-horse.—The name given by whalemen to a wad of muscles and tendons found in the tapering part of the whale and in the thicker portion of its flukes.

White-rope.—Manilla, and the ropes which do not require tarring.

White squall.—Burst of wind encountered off the African coast.

Whole top-sails.—Under whole top-sails; said of a ship sailing under top-sails without any reefs tied in them.

Who shall have this?—When provisions or other things are distributed, a man turns his back and asks "Who," &c.

Widows' men.—Formerly imaginary seamen entered in the books as A.B.'s for wages which were paid to the Widows' Fund.

Wift or waft.—A flag tied by a yarn in the middle of the fly, and hoisted as a signal.

Wild.—Said of a ship when she steers badly.

Willy-waws.—Whirlwind squalls encountered in the Straits of Magellan.

Winch.—A machine with toothed wheels and pawls, worked by a handle and used in discharging cargo, &c. Many winches are worked by steam.

Wind abeam.—Sailing with the wind blowing at right angles to the ship.

Wind and water.—A ship hit by a ball that penetrates her at the water-line, so as to make an aperture just above and just below the surface of the water, is said to be struck between wind and water.

Wind-bound.—The same as weather-bound.

Wind-gall.—A halo of light on the edge of a cloud, and reckoned a precursor of stormy weather.

Windlass.—A large barrel, revolved by handles, on the forecastle, and used in getting up the anchor. This was the old windlass. Now there are many patent windlasses worked by steam.

Windmill.—The name given to an apparatus that resembles the arms of a small windmill, fitted to the pumps, which are worked by the revolution of the arms. In the absence of steam no better device than this could have been invented for saving the cruel labour of long pumping.

Wind-rode.—The situation of an anchored ship that is swung by the wind instead of the tide.

Winds.—Beaufort's figures denote the force of the wind thus: 0 Calm. 1 Light air. 2 Light breeze. 3 Gentle breeze. 4 Moderate breeze. 5 Fresh breeze. 6 Strong breeze. 7 Moderate gale. 8 Fresh gale. 9 Strong gale. 10 Whole gale. 11 Storm. 12 Hurricane.

Windward ebb.—When the tide is setting out and the wind blowing in.

Windward flood.—When the tide is setting in and the wind blowing out.

Windward great circle sailing.—The putting of a ship, in a foul wind, on the tack that enables her to lie nearest to her destination when steering upon the track of a great circle.

Wing.—The part of the hold or 'tween-decks next the sides.

Wing and wing.—Said of a fore-and-aft rigged vessel when going dead before the wind with her canvas out on both sides of her.

Wingers.—Casks stowed in the wings.

Wing ship.—A ship on the extreme left or right of a column.

Wire-drawn.—Said of steam when the steam-pipe of a marine boiler is so contracted as to diminish the pressure of the steam upon the piston during its stroke in the cylinder.

With a will.—Heartily. To pull with a will is to pull your best.

Withe.—An iron with a ring attached to it for rigging booms through: as, for instance, a short topgallant mast fitted with a withe to enable a royal mast to be rigged up.

Wood-backing.—The planking behind the iron or steel plates of armoured ships.

Wooden.—An old name for ship's carpenter.

Wooden-wings.—A name for lee-boards.

Wood-locks.—Pieces of wood, sheathed with metal, fixed to the stern-post to prevent the rudder unshipping.

Wood-sawyer's clerk.—A term to denote ease and independence.

Woold.—To wind a piece of rope round anything.

Woolding.—A strong lashing tautened by the insertion of wedges.

Worked.—"I wore ship and *worked* for such and such a port," meaning, "I tacked and beat against the wind in order to reach the port." Also said of packages of drugs carefully examined in dock for any damage which may have occurred during the voyage.

Working.—A ship is said to be working when her timbers and planking strain so as to let in water.

Work up.—The phrase for punishing a crew by keeping them at work beyond the usual hours. Sometimes "Work their old iron up."

Worm.—A tool for withdrawing a charge from a gun.

Worming.—To fill up the hollows in the strands of a rope by coiling spun yarn around them.

Wreck buoy.—A buoy painted green to denote the whereabouts of a sunken wreck.

Wrecker.—One who lures a ship to destruction for the purpose of plunder. One who steals wrecked goods, &c., which have been washed ashore.

Wring.—To strain.

Wring-bolts.—Bolts which secure the planks to the timbers.

Wring staves.—Pieces of plank used with the wring-bolts.

X

Xebeck.—A vessel square-rigged forward and lateen-rigged aft.

Y

Yacht.—A pleasure-vessel.

Yard.—A spar across a mast to fasten a sail to.

Yard-arm.—The end of a yard.

Yard-arm and yard-arm.—Lying side by side in an engagement so close that the yard-arms touch.

Yard-arm cleats.—Pieces of wood on the yard-arms where the lifts and braces are, where the head earings are secured.

Yard on the cap.—The situation of a yard lowered as far as it will go down the mast.

Yard-rope.—A rope for sending yards up or down.

Yard-tackles.—Tackles attached to the lower yards for hoisting boats, weights, &c., in and out.

Yarn.—Threads of hemp or other stuff. Also a narrative.

Yaw.—When a ship's head is swung by the send of a sea so as to throw her off her course, she yaws.

Yawl.—A man-of-war's boat. Also a vessel rigged as a cutter, but carrying in addition a small sail at the stern called a mizzen.

Yaw-sighted.—One who squints.

Yaw-yaw.—Jack's definition of a Dutchman, "Any man who says yaw-yaw for yes."

Yellow admiral.—A retired post-captain not entitled to promotion because he has not served his time in the rank he retires from.

Yellow-flag.—Quarantine colours.

Yellow Jack.—The yellow fever.

Yeoman.—The man in charge of a store-room in a man-of-war.

Yoke.—A piece of timber or iron fitted to the head of the rudder athwartships. Used for steering a ship by a wheel placed forwards, or where a tiller cannot be used.

Young gentlemen.—The term by which midshipmen in the merchant-service are addressed.

Youngster.—A youth; a boy.

Yow-yow.—A small Chinese boat.

Yulohs.—Chinese oars.

Z

Zenith.—The zenith of a place is a point in the heavens immediately above that place.

Zenith distance.—An arch of a vertical circle contained between the object and the zenith.

Zodiac.—A space in the heavens extending about 8° on each side the ecliptic.

Appendix

A ship's sails

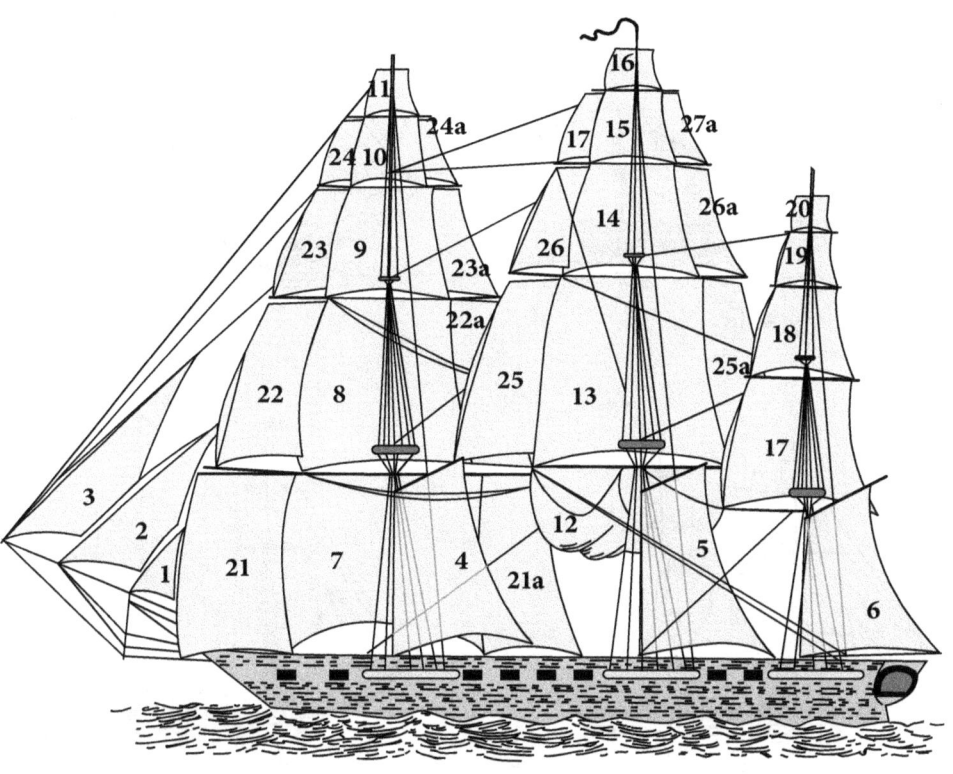

1. Fore topmast staysail
2. Jib
3. Flying jib
4. Fore spencer
5. Main spencer
6. Spanker
7. Foresail
8. Fore topsail
9. Fore topgallant sail
10. Fore royal
11. Fore skysail
12. Mainsail
13. Main topsail
14. Main topgallant sail
15. Main royal
16. Main skysail
17. Mizzen topsail
18. Mizzen topgallant sail
19. Mizzen royal
20. Mizzen skysail
21. Lower studdingsail
21a. Lee ditto
22. Fore topmast studdingsail
22a. Lee ditto
23. Fore topgallant studdingsail
23a. Lee ditto
24. Fore royal studdingsail
24a. Lee ditto
25. Main topmast studdingsail
25a. Lee ditto
26. Main topgallant studdingsail
26a. Lee ditto
27. Main royal studdingsail
27a. Lee ditto

Four types of ship

Ship   Barque

Full-rigged Brig   Hermaphrodite

Ship—A ship is square-rigged throughout; that is, she has tops, and carries square sails on all three of her masts. (*See page 118.*)

Barque—A barque is square-rigged at her fore and mainmasts, and differs from a ship in having no top, and carrying only fore-and-aft sails at her mizzenmast. (*See page 19.*)

Brig—A full-rigged brig is square-rigged at both her masts. (*See page 29.*)

Hermaphrodite brig—An hermaphrodite brig is square-rigged at her foremast; but has no top, and only fore-and-aft sails at her mainmast. Hermaphrodite Brigs sometimes carry small square sails aloft at the main; in which case they are called *brigantines*, and differ from a *Full-rigged Brig* in that they have no top at the mainmast, and carry a fore-and-aft mainsail instead of a square mainsail and trysail. (*See page 69.*)

www.ingramcontent.com/pod-product-compliance
Lightning Source LLC
Chambersburg PA
CBHW081352040426
42450CB00016B/3412